Expanding the Category "Human"

# Expanding the Category "Human"

*Nonhumanism, Posthumanism,
and Humanistic Psychology*

Patrick M. Whitehead

LEXINGTON BOOKS
Lanham • Boulder • New York • London

Published by Lexington Books
An imprint of The Rowman & Littlefield Publishing Group, Inc.
4501 Forbes Boulevard, Suite 200, Lanham, Maryland 20706
www.rowman.com

Unit A, Whitacre Mews, 26-34 Stannary Street, London SE11 4AB

British Library Cataloguing in Publication Information Available

**Library of Congress Cataloging-in-Publication Data Available**
Library of Congress Control Number: 2017956680
ISBN: 978-1-4985-5935-5 (cloth : alk. paper)
eISBN: 978-1-4985-5936-2

∞™ The paper used in this publication meets the minimum requirements of American
National Standard for Information Sciences Permanence of Paper for Printed Library
Materials, ANSI/NISO Z39.48-1992.

Printed in the United States of America

To my Parents,
George and Patti Whitehead

# Contents

# Foreword

From the Buddha in India to Anaximander in Greece, key thinkers in the ancient world came to recognize that temporality, and thus impermanence, was the hallmark of existence. Yet this deep lesson must ever be relearned anew, in each context. This book, by a young scholar, offers us older ones once again this challenge, this opportunity. It is an artful and deliberate provocation, a chance to go beyond what has been, to what might become. In this case, it is the discipline of psychology, understood as an approach to the human as human, that is set in transition. Patrick Whitehead knows the traditions and sources of humanistic psychology well. And, as he vigorously attests, his goal is not to abandon them, but to vivify them anew. For us "older ones" we might wince (indeed we do wince) when we see a cherished idea cast into an unsympathetic light. We might (yes, we do) even feel a concern that a prized notion is taken up ungenerously. The inevitability of impermanence does not make it any easier.

But that is the way of change. The younger generation advances the discipline, with little regard to the immense difficulty of the attainment of the hard-won turf so treasured by the previous, because it was not their battle that won such turf. In psychology of course this means the successful humanistic re-opening of the place of the human *as* human after its long exile by the behaviorist regime. To establish this space for the human was undoubtedly the most important accomplishment of the humanistic revolution of the latter twentieth century in American psychology, and those of us who lived it know just how difficult that was to achieve. And so any hint of ungenerosity in appreciating the details of that paradigmatic shift are disconcerting.

Yet it would be equally ungenerous to view Whitehead's work in terms of its critique of the past. It is so much more than that. He really has advanced a significant and comprehensive vision of a much larger integration of contemporary thinking about the meaning of that ever-contentious question of sub-jectivity and objectivity. In light of recent technological advances in artificial intelligence, questions of the meaning of the human as human have once again become contestable, previous verities disturbed, and a confusing ca-cophony of viewpoints unleashed. But these questions are important not only because they are again timely; they are the perennial questions that ever underlie any real psychology: What *does* it mean to be human? What *is* subjectivity? What is the nature of the engagement of the subject with an object? What is an object? A major reason that psychology has failed to advance to its maturity has been its failure to develop the serious philosophi-cal base from which to truly build upon a deep comprehension of these issues. And, until it does so, it is doomed to continue merely pouring its old wine into new bottles.

So this is the import of Whitehead's work: to very deeply address this key underlying level, the very basis for the development of a mature psychology. And he comes to this task with a depth of philosophical vision and a clarity of understanding that makes possible the sort of genuine advances that occur perhaps once a generation. Drawing astutely on forward edge sources, many of which will be new to American audiences, Whitehead not only poses the key questions, he is engaged in working out innovative, integrative resolu-tions of conundrums that have so long haunted the discipline. And, as he rightly notes, these resolutions will infuse psychology with the conceptual tools needed for its continuing relevance in the twenty-first century. This will be the century in which the question of the whole – of subjectivity/objectivity -- becomes paramount as we grapple with astonishingly transformative tech-nological advances but also with an ecological crisis of unprecedented dan-ger. We need now, more than ever, to step up to this holistic vision. This book is a wonderful example that such a vision is possible, and that psychol-ogy can have a key role to play in its realization.

—Christopher M. Aanstoos
University of West Georgia and founding editor of
*The Humanistic Psychologist*

# Acknowledgments

I learned, after writing the acknowledgements for my dissertation, that it is customary to begin with the most important acknowledgement before working your way down. A mentor had read mine and reported that he had grown concerned because I hadn't mentioned the name of my advisor, and he was running out of paragraphs left to go! I had, of course, left my advisor for the end. I won't make that mistake this time around: I'll begin with the most important ones: Mom and Dad.

Thank you, Mom and Dad, for supporting me through graduate school with weekly phone calls, morale boosts, and warm thoughts. Thank you for your patience as I defined obscure terminology that I would then use to describe even more obscure problems with contemporary philosophy of science. Thank you for the thoughtful cards and care packages (Mom), and for taking seriously my arguments, for example, that education shouldn't be a series of blocks laid one atop the other, even when you whole-heartedly disagreed (Dad). Thank you for buying my books even though they don't make particularly good evening reading. And thank you for continuing to say that you were proud of me even though I continued to gather degrees that students infamously "can't do anything with." I couldn't have done any of it without you.

Thank you to my dissertation committee for demanding more than I thought I could do. This book began four years ago as a doctoral dissertation. It was a culmination of five or so years studying a form of psychology that grew out of the philosophical trends of the middle part of the twentieth century. After my proposal (attempt)—unofficial, as it were, as I hadn't completed all of the prerequisite coursework—my committee members stared blankly back at me and each repeated their version of "umm… that's been done before."

I had taken the education that I had already received from my faculty, and given it back to them in a one hundred page promise of what was to come. I talked about the promise of phenomenology in the field of psychology, and how it simply hadn't been taken up in earnest by mainstream psychology. It was, in short, what every phenomenologically oriented humanistic psychology had done before me. The difference was that I had incorporated some new "posthumanism" references. It was very *avant garde.* But instead of "Bravo," they said "we can't have this; you need to go further."

I went back to my small apartment I had been living in for the previous three years, and found the most audacious of the phenomenology commentaries that I owned—Renaud Barbaras's book on Merleau-Ponty's unpublished manuscript *Visible and the Invisible.* It was a book about which I had earlier said "he takes Merleau-Ponty a bit too far" over a glass of wine at a phenomenology conference mixer. But now I read it with a new purpose: what if he *hadn't* taken it far enough.

Despite already being quite radical in his brand of phenomenology, Merleau-Ponty always expressed a sense that his work had gotten stale—that phenomenology was due for a transformation. This is when I looked back at the discipline of humanistic psychology, and began taking seriously the criticisms of humanism advanced by the posthumanities. I wrote a new proposal to this effect, and five months later defended it in front of the same four committee members. They did not complain that it had been done before. Thank you to my dissertation committee members: Chris Aanstoos, Eric Dodson, John Roberts, and Hans Skott-Myhre. Chris was gracious enough to chair my original draft (and write the foreword to the present volume), and John is responsible for introducing me to the Posthumanities movement.

For the concerned reader who does not wish to read a verbatim transcription of something that can be tracked down on microfilm, be encouraged that very little remains of the original dissertation. Kasey Beduhn and the editorial staff at Lexington Books have been helpful to me in shaping my dissertation into a monograph. Thank you all for your help.

I began working on this manuscript after five years of graduate study in one of the few humanistically oriented departments of psychology in the world—one that had been designed more than fifty years ago by Abraham Maslow and Mike Arons, among others. It was here that I began my love-affair with humanistic theory, methodology, pedagogy, and philosophy. As my pro-humanistic position grew stronger, I felt an anti- position develop as well: I became antipharmacology, anticognitive behavioral, antineuroscience, and so on. Somehow the humanistic psychological discourse of openness to possibility, inclusion and acceptance of a variety of viewpoints, and basic trust in the intentions and nature of others had been replaced by rigidity, narrow-mindedness, and distrust. Were these growing feelings endorsed by humanistic psychology, or had I somehow missed the point?

As I began re-examining the foundations of humanistic psychology, it became clear to me that the climate within the greater discipline of psychology had changed considerably since the middle of the 20th century. More specifically, what it means to be a *human* has changed—that is, the human 1950s is not the same as the human 2010s. The metaphysical problems that psychologists faced sixty years ago are not the same ones we face today.

# Introduction

There is an important decision that faces humanistic psychology, a decision that concerns the future of the tradition as well as the possibilities of inter- and transdisciplinary collaboration. Here is the decision as I see it:

1. It may continue its sixty-year-old project of protecting the integrity of human beings, or
2. It may continue its sixty-year-old project of openness of inquiry and acceptance of human beings.

When it began, humanistic psychology could choose both of these. Now the conditions have changed and the tradition must choose between them.

I maintain that decision two is in the best interests of humanistic psychology, and more specifically, that making this choice will solve three problems that have emerged in the last sixty years—problems that wouldn't have made sense in 1960. At that time, choice one and choice two could be accomplished at the same time. A great deal has changed outside the hallways of humanistic psychology and these can no longer be accomplished simultaneously.

Problem one concerns the alleged dividing line between "human" and "nature." At the time of its inception, humanistic psychologists could be found arguing against the dominant scientific trends in biology, physics, medicine, and other natural sciences. These trends, which I will explain in more detail below, followed the assumptions of Newtonian mechanics. It was popular to think of living things as assemblages of mechanisms that obey certain pre-determined rules. Humanistic psychologists have (rightly) objected to this kind of reduction of their subject-matter (human beings). Since humans cannot be understood as assemblages of mechanisms, it is reasoned that they must get their own category. This results in two categories of being: a complicated "human" category and the mechanical "everything else" category, commonly referred to as nature. In an effort to preserve the integrity of "human being," humanistic psychologists maintain that this category has something extra, and thus cannot be understood within the category of nature. You might even imagine that the human category sits higher in importance than the category of nature.

But today, biologists commonly object to this kind of reduction of their subject matter as well, as do physicists and physicians. That is to say, nothing in the "less-sophisticated" category of nature can be reduced to assemblages of mechanisms. An impressive interdisciplinary special edition of the *Journal of Progress in Biophysics and Molecular Biology* was published in December 2015 that accomplishes precisely this point. In it, physicists, mathematicians, biologists, philosophers, and psychologists discuss themes familiar to those of humanistic psychology.

Meanwhile, and in service to protecting the integrity of the category of "human," humanistic psychologists maintain that there is still something special about being a human. This position, which made sense sixty years ago, has become something of an ethical obligation: to understand cells and organs by the same processes the same way that we understand humans would be to miss out on this something special. Ironically, this very position has resulted in the loss of something special: the recognition that humans are of nature (and not somehow outside of or above it). Ecological therapist Andy Fisher (2013) explains that by keeping humans separate from nature, humanistic psychology has made the practice of ecopsychology impossible. Following ecological philosopher David Abram (1995) and French phenomenologist Maurice Merleau-Ponty (1964/1968), Fisher argues that humans and nature comprise the same fabric, and that they cannot be deeply understood in separation. That is to say, it has become counterproductive to maintain the unique integrity of human being.

Problem two concerns the outright rejection of non-subjective forms of knowledge. Once again, humanistic psychology has emerged out of a climate of behaviorism in American departments of psychology. Whatever remained of the subjective forms of psychological inquiry passed down from James (1890) and Wundt (1897) were lost in the infinite tedium of Titchener's classical introspection (1910; Boring, 1953). In 1930, John Watson argued that there was no consciousness, and no reason to view the verbal reports that subjects gave as anything other than speaking behavior. The subjective viewpoint had been rejected.

At around the same time as Watson was writing *Behaviorism*, a collection of philosophers referred to as the Vienna Circle were passing a bit of scientific legislation themselves: the scientists should no longer consider phenomenal qualities of experience, but that they must only be concerned with the physical components of experience—those that could be quantified. Once again, it was believed that these physical components followed Newtonian logic.

Humanistic psychologists maintain that the subject's perspective of their experience *does* contribute important data that must be considered in an investigation—indeed, it is even the *most* important. This is particularly compelling in applied psychology (clinical and counseling) where the subject must inform any diagnosis or subsequent treatment. It was understood that emphasizing the subject's perspective gives *meaning* to the matter. This is important when it was believed that organic matter followed the rules of Newtonian mechanics. But once again, it is no longer believed that cells and tissue only interact through certain and predetermined laws of mechanics. Entire schools of biology—e.g., "biosemiotics," the eastern European school of theoretical biology—view organic phenomena as meaningful, intersubjective, contextual, and even intentional! To be sure, biosemioticians do not ask for subjective descriptions of experience, but their practice is deeply consonant with the foundations of humanistic psychology. Indeed, one of the earliest concepts, self-actualization, was proposed by a neuro-psychiatrist with training in medical biology (Goldstein, 1934/1995), and it was used to describe *organisms* and not necessarily humans.

Like Problem One, the de-facto rejection of non-subjective forms of inquiry limits the interdisciplinary possibilities of humanistic psychology. This is unnecessarily restrictive; it is as if there is nothing left to learn about the nervous system that cannot be learned through subjective awareness of experience. Furthermore, the de facto rejection of non-subjective forms of inquiry goes against a value that was once held in high esteem by humanistic psychologists: openness of inquiry.

Problem three concerns the de facto rejection of anything that challenges the mid-century definition of "human" (e.g., "nonhumanism" or "posthumanism"). In the middle of this past century, it was important to argue *against* the mechanization of human beings. There is more to being human than a certain collection of part-processes. At this time it was important to demonstrate that humans are not just biological machines, so anything that demonstrated this was good: Wertheimer's holistic perception; Goldstein's (1934/1995) holistic biology; Merleau-Ponty's (1945/1962) embodied consciousness, among others. Moreover, humans had experiences that had no place in mindless mechanisms: experiences like love, expressions like will and intention, a practice of ethics, and so on. Together, the holistic attributes along with those experiences unique to human being amounted to what is meant by the category of human.

Take love, for example. American behaviorist B.F. Skinner defines love as a learned behavior.

When two people meet, one of them is nice to the other and that predisposes the other to be nice to him, and that makes him even more likely to be nice. It goes back and forth, and it may reach the point at which they are very highly disposed to do nice things to the other and not to hurt. And I suppose that is what would be called "being in love." (in Kohn 1993, p. 3)

Such a description seems absurd to somebody who has experienced love first-hand. This is not to say that Skinner's account isn't accurate in many important ways, it just misses out on an extremely important part: the meaning. It was assumed at the time that this extra "meaning" was something that the extra special "human" category contributes. That means that a human-human love is necessarily more meaningful than a human-machine love—like my love of my orange 2005 Honda: my Honda just cannot provide the kind of reciprocity that my wife does. The same may be said of me and my Australian Shepherd.

Note: it was the meaning as expressed by the subject that indicated that there is more to love than Skinner had described it. Instead of recognizing that the meaning found in human-dog or human-machine love is simply *different* from that of human-human love, it finds a place of privilege—much like what has happened with the category of human in Problem One. Today that privileging remains despite a noticeable shift social relations—a shift recognized by technologist and father of virtual reality Jaron Lanier (2009) and social media expert Sherri Turkle (2012). Lanier and Turkle both observe that human beings are beginning to rely more and more on technology to mediate their social interactions. They are also both very clear that this is a bad thing. Throughout this book I argue that these are merely different: the relationships mediated by digital technology today are merely different from those without this mediation sixty years ago. They are different, not deficient.

The privileging of the human category has become so strong that it has become customary to *deny* the first-person perspective of the subject who reports that she or he prefers online dating to face-to-face dating (a style we would do well not to call "actual" dating). If the human subject reports that he or she privileges a digitally-mediated relationship to a non-digitally-mediated relationship, it divides the humanistic psychologist in half! Fidelity to the subject or fidelity to the category "human"? The decision is an easy one: trust the subject. This requires the recognition that what it means to be a human has changed over the last sixty years. So rather than rejecting the emergence of the posthumanities, humanistic psychologists can join in, and do so in fidelity to their traditions of openness of inquiry and acceptance of human beings.

# HUMANISTIC PSYCHOLOGY

Humanistic Psychology began as a movement of American clinical psychologists who felt that the psychology they had been taught, and were subsequently expected to practice, was too limiting. Humanistic psychology was the answer to a psychology that seemed to leave its subject matter—namely, the human—behind. The title would seem redundant except for the culture of psychology out of which it emerged: behaviorism. Behaviorists were not interested in getting tied up with the question of what it means or feels like to be human. Indeed, to the behaviorists, psychology could be understood through man and animal alike.

Following the behaviorism of John Watson and B.F. Skinner, American psychology had achieved scientific status through its dependence on the experimental method. Behaviorism promised a science of behavior complete with experimental methods and a systematic and unambiguous approach to describing the subject matter of psychology. To the behaviorist, if it cannot be seen then it did not happen. Watson (1930) explains that the psychologist must rid herself with any interest in consciousness, feeling, understanding, dreaming, imagination, spirituality, and so forth. These, he argues, must be replaced with systematically empirical behaviors.

Abraham Maslow (1966)—a notable figure of this movement—describes how he had been disappointed with his top-tier education as a clinical psychologist. Like many at the time, the program at which he had been trained was a behaviorist one. He wondered how he would learn how to help people when all of his training had been with pigeons, rats, and dogs. After completing his doctorate, he had endeavored to practice a new kind of psychology—one that emphasized the *human*. While much of Maslow's early work was dedicated to a sort of psychological dualism—behaviorist psychology and humanistic psychology, he eventually began to argue that these both belonged to the same psychology.

In 1961, the *Journal of Humanistic Psychology* distributed its first publication, and the Association for Humanistic Psychology was developed two years later in 1963.

## Humanistic Psychology Calls for an Expansion of the Human in Psychology

Humanistic psychology makes a bold move by bringing human experience back into the realm of psychological inquiry.

Into the 1960s, the prevailing methods in psychology had been largely borrowed from the hard sciences of physics and physiology. These were the methods of experimentation that had already been tested and proven for several decades, and their validity and rigor was not in doubt. By their adoption, the young discipline of psychology would not need to forge its own methods, and could instead assert itself as a scientific discipline.

It is important to remember that psychology did not begin as an append-age of the hard sciences. Wilhelm Wundt (1897) and William James (1890) both describe methods that are distinct from those of physics and physiology in very important ways. These were the founders of psychology, but what they describe as the methods of psychology shares little in common with how it was being taught in the 1950s and 1960s.

Wundt argues for two aspects of psychological investigation, aspects he terms the "object of experience" and the "experiencing subject." The ob-jects—e.g., of physics—alone do not give you a psychology; an object does not cause your experience of it. The sense datum or stimulus does not give one sensation. To be understood psychologically, the stimulus must be viewed alongside the subject's experience of the stimulus. This two-part approach to psychology is unusual because Wundt is often remembered only for his experimental work in psychology (Toulmin & Leary, 1985).

William James describes a psychology of what he calls "radical empiri-cism." Recognizing how, by definition, empirical data must be gathered through the human senses, it is to the experience of these sensations that James turns. He explores memory, habit, emotion, imagination, instinct, will, and so on. Instead of operationally defining these in reductive and measur-able forms, James allows them to take form through a careful analysis of their subjective descriptions. He was listening to, even "trusting," the subject.

In the first two decades of psychology's growth as a separate discipline, two important things happened that would dictate the chosen methodology for the next century. First, the methodological trend was in favor of experi-mentation. Psychologists would dissect, test, and measure their subjects—often animals—in their research. James's dissatisfaction with associationist psychology—the psychology that would become popular in the first several decades of the twentieth century—can be seen in his *Principles of Psycholo-gy* (1890/2007) where he calls it "*psychology without a soul*" (p. 1). James also shares Wundt's disappointment with the direction psychological re-search appeared to be headed, which he calls "relatively insignificant by-products, and by no means the important thing" (in James, 1899, 10f).

The second important event that sealed psychology's fate as an experi-mental discipline was how Wundt's method for exploring the experiencing subject had been taken up by E.B. Titchener. Titchener was an American psychologist who had a laboratory devoted to, and was widely considered the expert on, Wundt's method of introspection (which centered on the subject's awareness of experience). In his historical account, Edwin Boring (1953) explains how the practice of introspection eventually became meaningless—nothing more than "a dull taxonomic account of sensory events which, since they suggest almost no functional value for the organism, are peculiarly uninteresting to the American scientific temper" (p. 174).

The result of these was the unquestioned acceptance of experimentation as the method for psychological research. In the United States, where humanistic psychology would soon blossom, this resulted in Behaviorism as the science of behavior, and neuro-physiology as the way of collecting data from subjects without having to take their word for it. Methodologically, the subject was slowly moving further and further away from the psychologist. Indeed, the latter would not have to talk to a single subject during data collection.

For Watson (1930), psychology as the science of behavior meant that there was no reason to bother with experiential constructs such as consciousness or feelings. Since they did not lend themselves of third-person empirical observation (that is, they could not be seen or measured), then they were make-believe and pseudo-psychological constructs. Around the same time, neuropsychologist Karl Lashley (1930) was recognizing a trend in clinical psychology to equate every quality of experience with the brain. Like James, Lashley saw this as an attractive, albeit ill-informed, development in the growth of psychology.

Measuring behavior or monitoring the brain. This is what humanistic psychologists stood up against. They argued that human experience cannot be eschewed without missing out on something important, so they set out to develop methods to once again open up the breadth of Wundt's original proposal. While psychologists were busy inventing new ways to study a subject without talking to her, humanistic psychologists began listening to their subjects.

Humanistic psychologists found the psychology of behaviorism too limiting. They called for an expansion of the subject matter from behavior to the person behaving. In this, human behavior is *included*, but so is the whole range of human experience. Transpersonal and Humanistic Psychology scholar Stanley Krippner explains:

> Where behaviorism emphasized observable behavior and applied technology, humanistic psychology focused upon (1) the *human beings* who behave (behavior is not excluded, but human beings are not reduced to their behaviors, (2) *human science* that adapts the method to the subject matter rather than the reverse, and (3) a *praxis*—or applications—that call for the real-world extension (both technological and non-technological) fo the conceptual structures created by humanistic theory. (vi-vii)

Humanistic psychology does not *reject* behaviorism, but finds the latter too limiting. As such they called for a broadening of the horizons of psychology.

This broadening can also be seen in Maslow's *Toward a Psychology of Being*. The introductory section is titled "A Larger Jurisdiction for Psycholo-

gy." He combines the insights of Goldstein's (1934/1995) biological observations of self-actualization with the philosophy of European existentialism.
Together they call for a psychology of process. The human being (and her
behavior), is not merely the sum total of parts that are present. She is not
merely the result of environmental stimuli, or a scientific object. She is an
ongoing process of being—of actualizing potentials. Maslow calls this self-
actualization, and Carl Rogers (1961) calls this becoming a person.

By recognizing that a person is both the object of behavioristic psychology *and* a process of becoming, they expand the jurisdiction of psychology to
include a much broader range of human experiences and existential meaning.
This expanded human is no longer a mere object for laboratory examination,
but may be found relating to their friends and loved ones, making marriage
plans, worrying about their career path, or building furniture. This is the
human that humanistic psychologists wanted to return to the domain of
psychology, the human that had been lost in the mechanization and reduction
of biological and behaviorist psychologies.


## POSTHUMANISM


Posthumanism supplies for the humanities what humanistic psychology has
supplied for the discipline of psychology in the middle of the past century: an
opportunity to expand the subject-matter. Posthumanism is an interdisciplinary field of study in the humanities that has only emerged out of the last few
decades. Also like the humanistic psychologists of the 1950s and 1960s,
posthumanists maintain the position that an important part of nature is being,
and has historically been, ignored in contemporary research.

In her book, *The Posthuman*, feminist philosopher Rosi Braidotti (2013)
describes a scene that captures the problem out of which posthumanism has
grown. The scene takes place at an early twenty-first century scientific meet-
ing of the Dutch Royal Academy of the Sciences.

> [A] professor in the Cognitive Sciences attacked the humanities head on. His
> attacks rested on what he perceived as the two major shortcomings of the
> humanities: their intrinsic anthropocentrism and their methodological national-
> ism. The distinguished researcher found these two flaws to be fatal for the field
> which was deemed unsuitable for contemporary science and hence not eligible
> for financial support by the relevant Ministry and the government. (p. 10,
> italics original).

The humanities are anthropocentric. Like using the adjective "humanistic"
before psychology, anthropocentric humanities sounds redundant. It is unsur-
prising that the humanities would have a narrow interest on the world as it
matters to humans. The humanities: studies of art, music, culture, literature,

dance, writing—are uniquely human ventures. When left unexamined, it would remain assumed that the arc of humanities scholarship must continually come back to itself. That's been done before—over and over and over again. "Humanism's restricted notion of what counts as the human is one of the keys to understand how we got to a post-human turn at all" (Braidotti, 2013, p. 16).

Such thought has prompted the question: what if there is more to the humanities than humans? To be sure, humans write stories, but are such stories the exclusive product of human factors? For dozens of generations, stories were told through song. Once words could be recorded on scrolls, is it possible that this *changed* the way stories were shared? It would seem so. In Europe, the new limitation on story recording and sharing put the process in the hands of a select few. For many centuries, it was the clergy who were responsible for which stories were shared and distributed. Such a detail is invisible when it is assumed that story sharing is a human activity that has been going on forever. That perspective ignores how the technology of sharing—be it oration, scrawled, print, or digital—fundamentally changes the *kinds* of stories that are shared, the *speed* of story-telling, and the *forms* of listening. The differences are not arbitrary, they reflect important posthuman influences.

Posthumanism is the study of the world after humans. This is immediately implied in the term itself. But what is not implied is precisely how it comes *after*. Posthumanism requires humanism. Like humanistic psychology being defined as that which covers the psychology missed by behaviorism, posthumanism catches that which is missed by the humanities. It examines what most humanities scholars forget to look at—like how the packaging of words changes the ways stories are shared. Posthumanism does not go back to the study of that which preceded the humanities, but builds on the kinds of scholarship already produced within their disciplines. Instead of eschewing the last century of humanities scholarship, posthumanism uses their methods, insights, and even questions. These are each slightly modified so that the subject matter is no longer anthropocentric. In this capacity, the posthumanities are post-humanities.

Posthumanism is post-human in another way, too: it recognizes that humans have created technology, and that technology has changed what it means to be human. The development of technology can only come by way of humans—that is, it depends on and is after humans. The wild-caught fish that my wife and I routinely eat depends on a variety of technological advances, not the least of which is refrigeration. Several innovations between ocean fishing to kitchen preparation are required in this culinary hobby of ours. Thus, culinary art continues to change in the direction of technology which is sometimes arbitrarily confining—like the size ratio of freezer-to-refrigerator in standard kitchen appliances. Crisper size and shelving limit the number of heads of raw cabbage we can keep, and preclude the keeping of entire deer carcasses. But how much of the culinary arts examines these limitations imposed by technology?

How technology has changed human communication, discourse, cognition, and lifestyle is studied by postphenomenology, which is described at greater length in chapter 7. Building on the phenomenological analyses of Don Ihde (1990), postphenomenology adds an important element to the phenomenologies of Husserl, Heidegger, and Merleau-Ponty. Rather than taking for granted that human consciousness is the nexus through which all meaning must be found and that it must be studied to the exclusion of all else, postphenomenologists emphasize that consciousness cannot go unchanged by the lifeworld. Increasingly, technology is a part of this lifeworld that persons share, so the transformations to consciousness are generalizable phenomena. For example, with its rise in popularity and accessibility, social media is becoming an increasingly common experiential theme. Postphenomenology would not merely ask for the subjective descriptions of the experiences of these social media outlets, but begin to examine their structure and function (in both virtuality and actuality). Doing so captures the way in which new pieces of technology transform humans in intended and unintended ways.

While postphenomenology uses an agreed-upon method for its research, not all posthumanities scholarship does. The very mentality of beginning without a set method allows scholars to break outside of the predictable patterns of the subject matter that they had learned from their predecessors, however comfortable and acceptable these may have been. For example, Graham Harman studied under Alphonso Lingis, a well-known phenomenology scholar at Penn State. Instead of continuing the work of his mentor, celebrating the great continental philosophers from the middle of the century in the same spirit, Harman advanced a (what was then) perverse reading of Martin Heidegger. Heidegger's famous work, *Being and Time*, is divided into two sections (it was originally supposed to be six, but only two were ever completed). The first section is a careful description of a method for understanding what it means for something to be there—Heidegger's ontological hermeneutic. The second section is an application of this method: understanding the structure of human being through the experience of one's death (in anticipation). Because of its application to the existential boundary of life, Heidegger is often read as an existentialist. Harman (2002/2006) suggested that Heidegger could just as easily have applied his method to understand the being of rebar, self-winding watches, and snow owls.

Harman went rogue. He challenged the common tendency in continental philosophy, which was to stay very close to what the original scholars had done. Phenomenology could only proceed in very small, careful, and methodical steps, and these steps must be approved by the original work of Husserl himself. This came as a breath of fresh air to young continental philosophy scholars who wished to apply the analyses in new and exciting ways. Sparrow would later argue that the traditional and conservative movement of phenomenology led to its own demise. But with Harman, phenomenological philosophy expanded exponentially.

Harman called his new take on Heidegger "object-oriented ontology." Instead of obsessing over human experience, it examined those things that had lain dormant for the centuries of modern thinking: objects. No longer passive to the experimenter's microscope, Harman's objects took on a participatory role that only phenomenologists could appreciate. The renewed appreciation of objects was not in the 17th century spirit of Newtonian mechanics, but in an exciting revitalization of things. This movement took several forms and applied a variety of methods, and it loosely fell beneath the moniker of "Speculative Realism" (Bryant, Srnicek, and Harman, 2011).

Speculative realists were not only experimenting with novel methods and subjects of study, they were also experimenting with new mediums of expression. For decades, the primary vehicle for sharing research in the humanities (as well as the social sciences) has been research monographs and published articles. These methods of idea sharing have the advantages of rigorous peer review, tradition, social validity, and professionalism. However, they have the tremendous disadvantages of being prohibitively expensive and frustratingly slow. It is not uncommon for research monographs to fall outside of the price-range for the interested reader or scholar, and to instead be purchased only by library collections. And unless one has the membership credentials, research articles can cost twenty or thirty dollars. Finally, the cutting-edge research article that is published in 2017 has probably been written in 2014, when it was on the cutting-edge. Almost by accident, the speculative realists transformed this process. Many of their leading scholars kept (and still keep) online blogs—which are like self-published personal journals, as well as a regular social media presence. Ideas spread immediately instead of having to wait the obligatory two to three year period. Journals—*O-Zone* for work inspired by Harman's object-oriented ontology and *Speculations* for work in speculative realism—are open-access and online, which means that they can be read without a costly association membership or university library card (assuming, of course, the university library has the desired subscription).

These solutions are not perfect ones, but they reflect an important theme in the posthumanities: the courage to challenge tradition in a variety of ways. The value of the scholarship can be determined after its fruit has been yielded.

Once the posthumanist's sort of questions become customary, the gaze of the humanities scholar can start to look at the impact that humans have had on the world in ways that don't necessarily translate back into the impact on humanity. Deforestation is not simply a problem because its continuation might impact the quality and breathability of the air for future generations of humans, but because habitats of plants and animals are being destroyed. And the extinction of an animal matters even beyond the fact that no human will ever be able to see one alive again. These impacts are posthuman: they follow human action, but they matter to more than humans and often do so in not-so-human ways. Philosopher Cary Wolfe edits a book series at Minnesota University Press titled *Posthumanities*.

Chapter 5 describes a few examples of what humanistic psychology research might look like if it were to adopt a posthuman perspective. It is maintained that doing so would not require the loss of the spirit of humanistic psychology, but even encourages its continued growth and applicability.

## NONHUMANISM

If posthumanism is the study of the nature *after* humans, nonhumanism is the study of nature *before* and without humans. Posthumanism requires the interaction of humans that continues to develop nature in new, not-specifically human (that is, posthuman) ways. "The nonhuman turn, on the other hand," Richard Grusin (2015) explains, "insists… that 'we have never been human' but that the human has always coevolved, coexisted, or collaborated with the nonhuman—and that the human is characterized precisely by this indistinction from the nonhuman" (p. ix-x).

The nonhumanists believe that there is nothing special about humans. Humans are simply part of a much larger, far more complicated system of interrelationships that preceded them and will continue long after they are gone. The study of human being is no different from studying any organic or biological process: the same tendencies, potentials, and possibilities exist. Moreover, these qualities do not belong to the human.

At first this sounds like the behaviorism that humanistic psychologists were arguing against, but this would be a mistake. Behaviorism borrowed its methodology from the reflex theory in physiology: a modern physics "cause→effect" relationship of behaviors. Modern physics was but one iteration of investigation into the nonhuman world of physical things. The unidirectional arrow of causality has been replaced with any number of concepts of causality in the last 130 years. Behaviorism, as behaviorists, zoologists, biologists, cognitive psychologists, and humanistic psychologists have each shown, fails because it takes for granted that behaviors can be isolated as part processes from the rest of the organism.

Kurt Goldstein was a neuropsychiatrist who had trained in the prevailing cause→effect reflex theory of the nervous system. However, in his research he could never seem to isolate behaviors from the overall functioning of the organism. Even the classic patellar tendon reflex could be inhibited if the environment demanded organismic excitation elsewhere. Goldstein challenges the prevailing medical models and called for a holistic biology that takes the entire organism (and its environment) into question before determining disease, symptom, or treatment.

Humanistic psychologists (Maslow, Perls, and others) were rightly inspired by Goldstein's work, and began using his concept of "self-actualization" to describe the perfectly natural process of becoming an individual (that is, a self-regulating organism). When Goldstein introduced the term, he was describing a nonhuman process that applied to a variety of life-forms. However, when Maslow used the term, he was describing a uniquely human process.

Self-actualization is not behaviorist. Behaviorism misses the tendency of an organism toward self-actualization because the former is too focused on discrete behaviors that do not betray holistic meaning. Humanistic psychologists were correct in using Goldstein's work to eschew behaviorism. The latter misses out on any holistic insights that contribute to the meaning an experience may have for an individual. This is a nonhuman principle in which humans share. It is not the unique domain of human being, but applies to all organic processes (as Goldstein has argued).

Grusin explains two important axioms of nonhumanism. Following the philosopher Brian Massumi, he calls the first one the study of affect systems. "Affect systems operate autonomously and automatically, independent of... cognition, emotion, will, desire, purpose, intention, or belief—all conventional attributes of the traditional liberal humanist subject" (p. xvii). This sounds an awful lot like Watson's list of taboo terms for psychologists. Since they are concepts that are often used to describe human experience, humanistic psychologists may be reluctant to let them go. But it is important to remember that the popular humanistic concept of "self-actualization" came from such a vantage point.

The second axiom is that "affectivity belongs to nonhuman animals as well as to nonhuman plants or inanimate objects, technical or natural" (Grusin, 2015, p.xvii). That is to say, nonhumans examine the processes of living and nonliving things, and humans can be explored as processes in both of these capacities.

## CARRY-OVER

Another concept that will play an important role in this book is that of "carry-over." Carry-over is the tendency to hang onto an element of a belief system, worldview, or paradigm even after these belief systems, worldviews, or paradigms have been dispensed with. This is particularly important for humanistic psychology since the latter has argued *against* the practice of reducing persons to mechanical assemblages. It is not enough to divide a person into the smallest measurable units, however convenient this might be to the methods of objective science. However, the attempts to correct this, humanistic psychology has carried over the problematic subject-object relationship, though they have reversed the privilege in the relationship.

Philosopher Ivor Leclerc introduces this concept in the essay he delivered at an interdisciplinary science and philosophy conference in Bellagio, Italy in June, 1974. The conference was organized around the question, popular among scholars of Alfred North Whitehead, of whether mind belonged uniquely to humans or if it could be generalizable to physical objects and biological organisms as well. Leclerc explains how the outright rejection of mind in physical matter was a customary assumption among scientists many centuries ago. Matter, it was assumed, was passive: like a billiard ball awaiting the contact of the cue ball. This behavior is much different from the agentive activity of the billiards player. However, this concept of physical matter has undergone many transformations since the seventeenth and eighteenth centuries. The continued belief that activity belongs to subjects while passivity belongs to objects is no longer tenable; it has no place in contemporary experimentation.

That the position—physical matter is mindless, passive, ineffectual—is still maintained today seems to be more of an example of the phenomenon of habit among researchers than as a manifestation of its explanatory efficacy. "To become clear about that conception" Leclerc (1977) explains, "is also important because there is still a very considerable carry-over of features [...] which are inconsistent with the new conception of the physical now requisite and in our time in the process of formulation" (p. 101).

American psychologist and theoretical physicist Steven Rosen identifies another instance of carry-over when he describes the shift from classical physics to contemporary physics (2008). Classical physicists have operated under the assumption that the important stuff happened in-between objects while the scientists (the perceiving subjects) could stand idly by. In the arena of classical physics, action potency and ontological privilege belonged to objects. However, during the quantum turn that relationship reverses. Physicists realize that they cannot observe the quantum objects without interfering with them. Electrons move so quickly that their location and speed cannot be predicted unless they are hit with another electron, and in this case you have interfered and still don't know the electron's speed.

Wont to acknowledge the role played by the subject (scientist in this example), physicists began to wonder how significant that role is. In an extreme example, Henry Stapp (2011) explains that all of these quantum phenomena can be understood as a universal mind.

Even though the quantum turn has required a substantial revision of the relationship between physical objects and observing subjects, contemporary physics *carried-over* the idea that one has to be more important than the other. There was no reason to keep this assumption other than precedent.

Carry-over is an important concept in the present work because it can be useful in helping understand the habitual tendency to reject certain methods of investigation. Humanistic psychologists (as well as biologists and physicians) have decried the severe restrictions imposed by neurological associationism, reflex theory, and the philosophy of mechanism that were issued by modern biological theory at the close of the nineteenth century. However, biological theory has changed significantly since then, and it will be argued that much of the outright rejection of these advances by humanistic psychologists can be explained by carry-over.

## Using the Ethics of Spinoza to Avoid Carry-over in Humanistic Psychology

Instead of merely reversing the relationship between objects and subjects in psychology, they must be transformed by an entirely new system. For that I recommend the *Ethics* of Spinoza (2000). While Newton and Galileo, relying on Aristotle's efficient causality, began describing a world of independent objects that related in predictable and manipulatable ways, Spinoza had described a world whose object-relations weren't as easily predicted in advance. Instead of assuming from the outset that objects must relate to one-another along predictable axes of spatial and temporal causality, Spinoza observed object relations in a way that opened them up to greater possibilities of becoming (and not mere unidirectional linear causality as required by efficient causality). Spinoza referred to this form of causality as "reason or cause." Consider, as an example, the relationship between an isosceles triangle and its angle-measures, as it is described by French philosopher and Spinoza scholar, Gilles Deleuze (1970/1988):

> In this case, one is not saying that first there is an isosceles triangle, and then there is a triangle whose base angles are equal; rather, the reason involved here is the timeless one of logical relationship. To say, then, that God is "cause of himself" is not to say that God first exists and then brings about his own existence; it is to say that God's existence follows logically from the concept of God. (p. 28)

Deleuze unpacks this double-meaning of causality:

> A finite existing thing refers to another finite existing thing as its cause. But it will not be said that a finite thing is subject to a dual, horizontal and vertical, causality, the first being constituted by the indefinite series of other things, and the second by God as to that which determines the cause to have its effect. (citing Spinoza, 1641, E1 P26; p. 54)

In his *Ethics*, Spinoza supplies a metaphysical framework that is radically divergent from the Newtonian framework that would receive the majority of attention in the development of the sciences. This is just one of the ways in which his alternative view of modernity is similar to the one that humanistic psychology has supplied for the modern practice of psychology. The similarities are abundantly evident when Spinoza is compared to the master existential-phenomenological psychotherapist, and famous fixture at the humanistic psychological institute, Esalen: Fritz Perls.

Spinoza and Perls each advocate an existence that is determined. This is evident in Perls's *Gestalt Prayer* where the difference between event *A* unfolding and event *B* unfolding is less of a matter of ego-intentionality than it is the sheer actuality of either event *A* or *B* unfolding. One's ego may have decided that event *A* is preferable to *B* and will resultantly hold on tightly to the hope that *A* will unfold. Perls has identified this ego ideal as the source of *anxiety*—which he terms "developmental disorder" (so as to distinguish it from neurosis or pathology). Similarly, Spinoza may be understood as identifying the same "attachment to one's ideas" as an instance of inadequate ideas—the least developed type of knowledge, which is always marked by sad passions. Though Perls and Spinoza have in mind a determined universe, this does not mean that one may as well give up on existence. Instead, what is advocated in both is the vibrancy and infinite possibility of being.

## SUMMARY OF CHAPTERS

Chapter One introduces what I have termed the Cult of Humanistic Psychology. In 1985, two historians of psychology (Toulmin & Leary) made the argument that psychologists have fallen into the trap they called the "cult of empiricism." Instead of embracing the breadth of Wundt's (1897) project of psychology—that is, objects of experience and the experiencing subject, psychologists have focused only on the things of experience and thus have ignored subjectivity. In their effort to correct this imbalance, humanistic psychologists have ignored the objects of experience. Following the project of the well-known humanistic psychologist Abraham Maslow (1962/1968), it is argued that humanistic psychology has worked its way into its own corner and has transformed a movement of openness and creativity into one of limitations and rigidity.

Chapter Two introduces the first problem that humanistic psychology must address: the alleged human-nature divide. By arguing against the dehumanization of humankind, humanistic psychologists have customarily maintained that humans are in a category of their own, and as such they deserve preferential treatment. This has led to an veneration of humankind no more anthropocentric than geocentrism. Subjectivity and consciousness are subsequently understood to be exclusively in the arena of humankind. Humanistic psychology relies heavily on methods derived from the continental philosophies (phenomenology and existentialism) that are guilty of a similar error. However, there is little evidence—in phenomenological philosophy or after—that humankind is more ontologically differentiable from the rest of nature. By dividing humankind from the rest of nature, humanistic psychology alienates its subject matter from its environment. This undermines the projects of clinical- and eco-psychology. Chapter Three describes how the division between humankind and nature can be dissolved, and discusses what this would mean for ecopsychology.

Chapter Four introduces the second problem that must be addressed: the rejection of nonhuman forms of subjectivity. By closely following the ontological foundations of existentialism and phenomenology, humanistic psychology finds humans at the nexus of meaning in the universe. Nineteenth century objectivitivism is shunned while the human vantage point is celebrated in its noetic singularity. This vastly limits the scope of phenomenology to a method of anthropocentrism. However, the exclusive focus on noetic phenomenology ignores Husserl's hyletic phenomenology. In the not-yet-formed subject-object one finds a material phenomenology that satisfies Merleau-Ponty's (1964/1968) postphenomenological leanings.

Chapter Five outlines the advantages to merging humanistic psychology with the nonhumanities. Despite its principled stance that the psychological study of the human is in a class all of its own, humanistic psychology has historically relied on concepts that come from the natural sciences. Self-actualization is one such concept. Coined by medical biologist and holistic psychiatrist Kurt Goldstein, self-actualization is a behavioral organizing process that applies to all things. Indeed, the humanistic psychology of persons may be compared to the sign-interpretation of organic life in biosemiotics (Whitehead, 2017).

Chapter Six introduces the third problem that humanistic psychology must address: the de facto rejection of posthuman changes in human being. Remarkably, a mission to accept persons has resulted in the rejection of certain forms of being—specifically those mediated by technology. Sympathizers to the plight of humanistic psychology (Lanier, 2009; Turkle, 2012) cry afoul as they witness the transformation of humankind by advances in technology: online dating, text-messaging, video-psychotherapy, online teaching, and so on. Instead of an attitude of acceptance, one finds disappointment about what has been lost. In Chapter Seven it is argued that humanistic psychology can maintain its mission of openness to all possible posthuman varieties of being by using its methods to investigate them. Just like mid-century phenomenology has demonstrated the way the human body shapes consciousness, so too have contemporary phenomenologists demonstrated the way in which smart-phones, web-browsing, and online dating have transformed consciousness. These and other examples amount to a post-human psychology.

Chapter Eight investigates the radical edge of the proposed growth of the human category. If what is meant by "human" can extend to include traditionally nonhuman entities and processes, can the science of the human—namely, psychology—be extended to these nonhuman things? Following the object-oriented ontology of Graham Harman (2002/2006, 2005), a program for object-oriented psychology is designed.

The concluding chapter reminds the audience that expanding the category of the human is not a loss or a victory; it is simply a change. Special care is taken to explain how humanistic psychology is in a unique position to dialogue with the interdisciplinary movements of posthumanism and nonhumanism. As a scholar and teacher, I remain very much committed to the project of humanistic psychology, and wish to see its own potential actualized.

*Chapter One*

# The Cult of Humanism in Psychology

There is a trend in humanistic psychology that has become increasingly disturbing. I have decided to call this trend the "cult of humanism." Briefly, the "cult of humanism" typically defines itself in dialectical opposition to the positions of modern natural science—that is, against the ontological assumptions of logical empiricism and against the methodological procedures and analyses of controlled experimentation. Moreover, this cult insinuates an ethical imperative to the flat rejection of modern natural science. For the scientist who is having trouble sleeping at night: discard your SPSS reports and ask a person a penetrating, open-ended question.

Many examples from contemporary research in humanistic psychology might serve as a useful introduction to this chapter. Take, for instance, the article that I have written for the *Humanistic Psychologist* titled "Neuroscience Humanizes" (2014). In it I argue against the prevailing neural-reductionist approaches to the human, and maintain that the only fruitful models for making sense of the nervous system are the ones that recognize the subjective experiences of the humans in which they take part. This is because there exist a handful of anomalies in the linear associationist models of neuroscience that may be explained by subjective, humanistic-models of science. Humanists-1, neuroscientists-0. Moreover, there is a great richness and depth to non-humanistic models of neuroscience—ones that recognize all sorts of non-linear causation and systemic complexity—which has been completely ignored.

I have already presented three problems that humanistic psychologists face that have developed over the last sixty years. Before going into these in more detail, I would like to describe an exemplar of what I am calling "The Cult of Humanism." It is an exemplar that the audience of humanistic psychologists might find particularly irksome: Abraham Maslow—one of the founders and champions of humanistic psychology. To be sure, nothing that Maslow does is antihumanistic. Everything that he does is in service to the project of humanistic psychology. However, I argue that he has taken the axioms of humanistic theory too far and actually begins to undermine the entire project. Like Problems One, Two, and Three, Maslow's work becomes counterproductive to the aims of humanistic psychology. Instead of openness of inquiry, he demands that limitations be in place. In defending his tradition, I argue that Maslow leaves behind the philosophical and theoretical foundations of humanistic psychology. My hope is that a description of how this can happen will help others avoid doing the same thing.

## THE CULT OF HUMANISM

The familiarity of the title is not a coincidence. More than thirty years ago, two psychologists published a paper titled "The Cult of Empiricism..." (Toulmin and Leary, 1985). Toulmin and Leary do not argue that empiricism is bad. I cannot think of anybody who would argue that empiricism is bad. Empiricism is not the bad guy—*blind allegiance* to empiricism that *ignores* alternatives is the bad guy. Toulmin et al describe the increasingly problematic trend in psychology to practice a science that has been separated from its philosophical roots. In their rendition, the trend has been in favor of logical empiricism. This, the authors note, has been followed by a blind allegiance that is suggestive of cult practice. Their conclusion is an exhortation to the greater scientific discipline of psychology to keep an open dialogue with philosophical foundations. Nearly thirty years later I find that a similar warning must be issued.

Once again, "humanistic psychology" is not the bad guy. Indeed, I am very convinced that humanistic psychology has a great deal to offer psychology and interdisciplinary science in the rwenty-first century. However, I argue that it must recommit to endorsing the ever-changing human that gives it its name, as well as the project of expansion that it had from the outset (described in the Introduction). It is not humanity that must change to meet the needs of humanistic psychology, but the reverse. I wish to discuss three different examples of this: the separation of humans and nature, the rejection of posthuman forms of being; and the rejection of non-subjective and non-qualitative methodologies.

The problems that stem from the cult of humanism may be seen in the stigma that gets attached to practices that fall outside of those endorsed by the human-centric and holistic models of being. This stigma results in a counterproductive practice of humanistic psychology, demonstrated by Problems One, Two, and Three. The impact that these problems have on humanistic psychology will be carried out in the following three chapters.

The purpose for my selection of Maslow is threefold. First, Maslow (1966) has held the philosophical foundations of science in high-esteem—referencing, for example, the medical biology of Kurt Goldstein (1934/1995), the epistemology of Michael Polanyi (1958), and the history and philosophy of science provided by Thomas Kuhn (1962/2012). Second, Maslow has been a well-known contributor to, and progenitor of, the development of humanistic psychology, which is of obvious concern to the present project. And finally, Maslow has a wealth of provocative examples that span experimental and applied psychologies. A list to which one could easily add: he has been generally held in high esteem—a claim defended even by his younger, more traditional co-faculty members while he was at Brandeis (Lowry, foreword to Maslow, 1962/1998).

## FROM CREATIVITY TO CULT: MASLOW'S HUMANISTIC PROGRAM FOR PSYCHOLOGY

Consider the apt practice of humanistic psychology from the vantage point of Toulmin et al (1985): at issue is any practice of psychology that proceeds divorced from its philosophical roots. That is, without open dialogue regarding its assumptions. In this regard, Maslow's (1966) project of a human-centered psychology sets off admirably:

> If there is any primary rule of science, it is, in my opinion, acceptance of the obligation to acknowledge and describe all of reality, all that exists, everything that is the case. Before all else science must be comprehensive and all-inclusive. [...] At its best it is completely open and excludes nothing. It has no "entrance requirements." (p. 72)

Maslow countenances the psychological project of Wundt (1897) in all of its breadth. Objects, subjects, and their curious interstices are present to Maslow's psychology. In order for science to proceed in a manner that is connected to the continuing philosophical exploration that supports it, the former must remain open and accepting. No methodological position can hold *a priori* privilege over others. Maslow continues,

> This world of experience can be described with two languages, a subjective, phenomenological one and an objective, "naively realistic" one, as Niels Bohr pointed out long ago. Each one can be close to the language of everyday life, and yet neither describes life completely. Each has its uses and both are necessary.... (p. 45, footnote)

Notice that Maslow is careful to include that each science "has its uses and both are necessary." That is to say, a science that privileges phenomenology is just as incomplete as one that privileges associationism. Thus far, Maslow has introduced a psychological project no less encompassing and audacious than that of Wundt.

## Maslow Echoes the Cry against Mechanized Science

The middle of the twentieth century has contributed a great sum of criticism toward various forms of Bohr's aforementioned "naïve realism." Following the language the latter had received in biology (e.g., Goldstein, 1934/1995) and perception psychology (e.g., Köhler, 1947/1957), Maslow (1966) has called this a mechanistic approach to psychology. In a move that draws into question his efforts at unification, Maslow has polemically characterized mechanistic psychology as dehumanizing (which is understood to be a bad thing). He briefly explains this, as well as the humanistic response:

> But in this century, and especially in the last decade or two, a counter philoso-
> phy has been rapidly developing along with a considerable revolt against the
> mechanistic, dehumanized view of man and the world. It might be called a
> rediscovery of man and his human capacities, needs, and aspirations. These
> humanly based values are being restored to politics, to industry, to religion,
> and also to the psychological and social sciences. I might put it so: while it was
> necessary and helpful to dehumanize planets, rocks, and animals, we are real-
> izing more and more strongly that it is *not* necessary to dehumanize the human
> being and to deny him human purposes. (p. 2)

Maslow is keen on the aforementioned criticisms of a strictly logically em-pirical science. Moreover, he finds that nature herself has been subsequently drained of life—a desaturation that has occurred due to a mechanized con-ception of nature. However, instead of revivify Nature, Maslow indicates that revivification is only necessary for the human order. By making this argu-ment, Maslow effectively draws a line in-between humans and nature. More-over, he insinuates that the human category has something that nature does not.

In addition to the implicit anthropocentrism, what is important to note here for the present discussion is that a philosophy of mechanism, while appropriate for geodes, geography, and giraffes, loses something when it is used to understand humans. Maslow's open door policy for psychology gets restricted to holistic, correlationist, and humanistic methods.

## Maslow Misinterprets Polanyi's Critique of Naïve Realism as a Defense for Subjectivism

Polanyi's (1958) publication of *Personal Knowledge* has evidently had an impressive impact on Maslow (1966). Indeed, the former was extolled in the acknowledgements, preface, and body of the latter. The dual epistemology that Polanyi presents is certainly opposed to the billiard-ball realism that has been ridiculed throughout the century during which he wrote. Like Maslow, Polanyi criticizes the presumption that science is capable of investigating reality in any direct way. For example, Polanyi (1964) writes that "the ideal of exactitude has to be abandoned" (p. 10). More specifically, he argues that the methods of objectivity and probability are not as infallible as the logical empiricists maintain. These, Polanyi (1958) suggests, might be replaced with qualities no less essential to scientific inquiry—qualities he refers to as "personal knowledge," "intuition," and "conscience." This is where Maslow (1966) picks up the idea "that scientific knowledge is 'personal,' that it necessarily involves judgment, taste, faith, gambling, connoisseurship, commitment, responsibility" (p. 34, footnote).

Polanyi's insights are used as a source of epistemological inspiration for the work of Maslow. The problem arises when Polanyi's sophisticated realism is discarded for subjectivism—that is, an epistemological defense in favor of a singular focus on the human subject to the exclusion of all else.

> There is no substitute for experience, none at all. All the other paraphernalia of communication and of knowledge—words, labels, concepts, symbols, theories, formulas, sciences—all are useful only because people already know experientially. The basic coin in the realm of knowing is direct, intimate, experiential knowing. Everything else can be likened to banks and bankers [...] which are useless unless there is real wealth to exchange. (pp. 45-46)

Given Polanyi's (1958) impressive and systematic critique of the epistemological foundations of logical empirical scientific practice, Maslow's conclusion is understandable. Add to this Polanyi's suggestion that all inquiry requires a personal element, the position becomes quite clear indeed. But this is not Polanyi's conclusion.

Polanyi (1964) maintains that the starting point of science as one of perception. But he does so while maintaining a sophisticated realism. That is, Polanyi (1958, 1964) has critiqued naïve billiard-ball realism in order to propose a more sophisticated realism. He does so through two points: first, scientists cannot possibly be objective about the universe because the practice of inquiry (only four centuries old, and limited to what can be explored from Earth) has only investigated a microcosm of the geography of the universe in a very narrow and hyper-specific time-frame; second, scientists are always making personal judgments about the objects being investigated—which questions to ask, which tools to use, where to look, and so on. Together, these claims suggest that scientific practice is just as much personal as it is objective. After disabusing realism of Newtonian assumptions regarding objectivity, Polanyi (1964) develops a realism based on the insights of Gestalt Perception Theory. He argues that the world presents *itself* in particular ways, through particular and not arbitrary gestalts. This structure of things is available in a tacit-dimension, a dimension of communication between objects and subjects, mediated by intuition. That is, scientists do not access objects directly, but do so through the mediation of certain tools. The gestalt-structure of things, as Polanyi states above, *is in the aspects of reality* and not in the subject. "We know that perception selects, shapes, and assimilates clues by a process not explicitly controlled by the perceiver" (1964, p. 11). Thus, the importance of experience that might be gleaned from Polanyi is not in one's experience per se, but in the experience of the thing in question. Were one to collapse the dualism between subjects and objects onto one side of the divide, Polanyi would look to the objects and not to the subject. For Polanyi, essence belongs on the side of the real—the objects themselves—and not in the subject. He compares the process of science with that of artwork by indicating this important difference:

> The process resembles the creation of a work of art which is firmly guided by [the subject's] fundamental vision of the final whole, even though that whole can be definitely conceived only in terms of its yet undiscovered particulars— with the remarkable difference, however, that in natural science the final whole lies not within the powers of our shaping, but must give a true picture of a hidden pattern of the outer world. (1964, p. 32)

Polanyi's critique of naïve realism does not result in a rejection of all forms of realism; it instead defends a more complicated form. To be sure, this more sophisticated form makes it possible to speak of the validity of subjective claims about reality—something denied by naïve realism. Polanyi realizes that the role the scientist plays is of some importance and not merely arbitrary. However, instead of now viewing alternative forms of epistemological validity alongside modernist objectivity, Maslow has used these critiques of naïve realism to dismiss objective claims entirely. Objective claims are replaced with subjective claims, and the latter are limited to human subjects. In his survey of neuroscientific theories of consciousness, Alva Nöe (2009) suggests that, like Maslow's bankers above, objective correlates of consciousness are useless without their subjective engagement.

## Humanistic Psychology's Theory of Consciousness

With an anthology of anomalous neurobiological case-studies in one hand, and a celebratory humanitarian flag in the other, Nöe (2009) proudly proclaims that *You Are not Your Brain*. Nöe has compiled an impressive number of evocative examples how the Modernist conception of consciousness fails as a comprehensive system of explanation. After rejecting the primacy of the nervous system, Nöe defends the primacy of the embodied-subject:

[T]o understand consciousness in humans and animals, we must look not inward, into the recesses of our insides; rather, we need to look to the ways in which each of us, as a whole animal, carries on the processes of living in and with and in response to the world around us. The subject of experience is not a bit of your body. You are not your brain. The brain, rather, is a part of what you are. (p 7)

Noë explains that the mind/body problem is more difficult than simply picking a side. Heavily influenced by the phenomenology of Merleau-Ponty (1945/1962), Noë outlines an intentional consciousness that begins with the primacy of perception. Perception co-constitutes a subject and her environment. It is through perception that both subject (mind) and object (body) become. Like Merleau-Ponty before him, Noë comes dangerously close to defending an immanent causality where body and mind, subject and object are understood to be reciprocally effected-affecting. Instead, like Merleau-Ponty (*Cf.* Merleau-Ponty 1964/1968; Barbaras, 1991/2004) before him, Noë is found occupying a correlationist position. Look at the trip-up committed by Noë: "You are not your brain. The brain, rather, is a part of what you are." Backing up a few lines, Noë assumes the unified whole-animal designates the subject. Are we to imagine that subjectivity is thus relegated to whole animals? Or is it, perhaps, in the reverse? Instead of looking to the brain for a reductive definition of being, consciousness, and humanism, Noë has looked to the subject.

To be sure, the book is a compelling case for what can be learned, understood, and demonstrated about experience when neuroscience is undertaken as a project of humanistic psychology. But, like Crick (1994) and Koch (2012), Noë has limited the quest of understanding serendipity, infomercials, and bicycle gain-ratios to a single system of explanation: he has chosen the intentional embodied-subject to the neglect of neural correlates. Noë, along with the human-subjectivity-bound phenomenologists (Harman, 2011), have erected a universe around the assumption that the reality is either for human-subjectivities or, no less anthropocentric, may only be meaningfully understood through human subjectivity. In this sense, Noë's science of the embodied subject is no less limited in possibilities than is the modernist project of logical empiricism. *The complicated subject/object interrelationship that Noë has proposed is not inherently problematic, but when it in principle denies the utility of alternative conceptions of consciousness, it becomes dogmatic.* This is the problem. Additional problems arise when subjectivity is limited to certain entities. This will be explained in commentary to Maslow's interpretation of Goldstein, below.

## Maslow Insinuates an Ethic into Kuhn's Distinction between Scientists

It is understandable that the progenitors of a bourgeoning science might look to chemist-turned-philosopher of science Thomas Kuhn (1962/2012) for inspiration. Kuhn discusses the novelty, spontaneity, and creativity of the 'revolutionary' scientists on grounds equal to those of the accomplished, esteemed, and exacting 'normal' scientists. Maslow borrows Kuhn's distinction to defend his alternative approach to psychology as an instance of 'revolutionary' science, but he takes it too far in two ways. This occurs first when Kuhn's bipartisan distinction is used to attack the preceding scientific practices. Rather than recognizing their mutual importance, Maslow has assumed to have what amounts to an ethical edge on his immoral, modernist predecessors. It is taken too far a second time when I have assumed that the qualities of both types of scientist may be taken together—that is, the spontaneity and creativity of the 'revolutionary' along with the production of textbooks and graduate programs of the 'normal' scientists. Indeed, given the decades of publications, journals dedicated to its research, creation of graduate schools, and recognition by the APA, humanistic psychology is beginning to be more representative of Kuhn's normal sciences! In the present section, attention will be paid to the first instance. Discussion of the second instance may be found throughout the analysis of the restricted subject-matter—the topic of the following section.

In the middle of the century, Kuhn's 'normal' psychologists were the behaviorists. Maslow was surrounded and even trained by psychologists of the behaviorist ilk. George Miller describes the setting of American departments of psychology typical of this time:

> The chairmen of all the important departments would tell you that they were behaviorists. Membership in the elite Society of Experimental Psychology was limited to people of behavioristic persuasion; the election of the National Academy of Sciences was limited either to behaviorists or to physiological psychologists, who were respectable on other grounds. The power, the honors, the authority, the textbooks, the money, everything in psychology was owned by the behavioristic school. Those who didn't give a damn, in clinical or social psychology, went off and did their own thing. But those of us who wanted to be scientific psychologists couldn't really oppose it. You just wouldn't get a job. ... I would say up to the mid-'50s that was the situation. (in Baars, 1986, p. 203)

Miller describes in behaviorism, almost point-for-point, Kuhn's characteristics of 'normal' science. But Kuhn indicates that science is not limited to the influence of any single paradigm by introducing an important accompanying element to this:

Perhaps science does not develop by the accumulation of individual discoveries and inventions. Simultaneously, these same historians confront growing difficulties in distinguishing the "scientific" component of past observation and belief from what their predecessors and readily labeled "error" and "superstition." (p. 2)

By observing the reversal of dominant scientific systems throughout the history of modernity, Kuhn maintains the validity and value for alternative modes of scientific exploration. It is a form of scientific investigation that sees what the 'normal' scientists might miss. Kuhn suggests that these scientists are 'revolutionary.' Thus, in the 1950s, behaviorism was the leading psychological paradigm while the 'revolutionary' projects of cognitive and humanistic psychology were underway. Kuhn explains the development of such revolutionary projects:

In the absence of a paradigm or some candidate for paradigm, all of the facts that could possibly pertain to the development of a given science are likely to seem equally relevant. As a result, early fact-gathering is a far more nearly random activity than the one that subsequent scientific development makes familiar (p. 15)

The 'revolutionary' scientists are thus typically more open-minded, creative, and spontaneous, but necessarily have a difficult time establishing anything in principle. The openness and wonder characteristic of the 'revolutionary' movements in science may be contrasted with the maturity of the 'normal' scientists. Kuhn explains that the "Acquisition of a paradigm and of the more esoteric type of research it permits is a sign of maturity in the development of any given scientific field" (p. 11).

While the adjectives Kuhn has used seem to suggest that normal scientists are vanilla and revolutionary scientists are Neapolitan, it is clear that each is important to scientific exploration. Moreover, Kuhn's analysis defends the importance of psychologists who choose to resurrect concepts such as "consciousness" that the dominant paradigm had systematically eliminated from the psychologist's vocabulary (e.g., Watson, 1930). Kuhn's appeal to Maslow is understandable. However, instead of using Kuhn's bipartisan distinction between scientists, Maslow (1966) uses this as an opportunity for disparaging the 'normal' scientists:

To some extent, the distinction between Kuhn's normal scientist and his revolutionary one parallels the development from the adolescent to the adult male, or from immaturity to maturity. The boy's conception of what a man should be like is more embodied in the 'normal' scientist, the obsessional character, the practical technologist, than it is in the great creator. If we could understand better the difference between the adolescent's misconception of maturity and actual maturity, we should thereby understand better the deep fear of creativeness and the counterphobic defenses against it. (p. 35)

One immediately notices that Maslow has reversed Kuhn's observation that the 'normal' scientist represents the form that is most mature, and has introduced his own theory of personal development that hinges on deficiency and growth needs. As Maslow sees it, the normal scientist—protected by esteemed academic positions, privileged association ties and reputable academic presses—is neurotically afraid of failure. He continues, the 'normal' scientist is "overobsessional… immature" and, "stressing control," tends to

> exclude, to set up hurdles and to close doors, to be suspicious. He is apt to dislike lack of control in others as well and to dislike impulsiveness, enthusiasm, whimsicality, and unpredictability. He is apt to be cool, sober, and stern. He is apt to prefer toughness and coolness in science to the point of synonymizing them. (pp. 38-39)

In addition to his reversal of Kuhn's observation of maturity in scientific practice, Maslow has introduced a problematic psychological distinction between Kuhn's scientists. Not only is the 'normal' scientist incapable of creativity, but she is also a shallow, defensive, and troubled person—evidently forced to use the esteem associated with the more pedantic form of science to make up for her own personal underdevelopment. Maslow distinguishes the 'revolutionary' maturity with the 'normal' immaturity in his comparison of researchers A and B (which match 'revolutionary' and 'normal,' respectively).

> An obvious illustration supported by common sense experience might be this. Researcher A is really fascinated with schizophrenics (or white rats or lichens). Researcher B, however, is much more interested in manic-depressive insanity (or monkeys or mushrooms). We may confidently expect that Researcher A will (a) freely choose or prefer to study schizophrenics, etc., (b) work better and longer at it, be more patient, more stubborn, more tolerant of associated chores, (c) have more hunches, intuitions, dreams, illumination about them, (d) be more likely to make more profound discoveries about schizophrenia, and (e) schizophrenics will feel easier with him and say that he "understands" them. In all these respects he would almost certainly do better than Researcher B. But observe that this superiority is in principle far greater for acquiring experiential knowledge than it is for acquiring knowledge about something, or spectator knowledge, even though Researcher A probably could do a bit better at that, too. (p. 51)

In review, to Kuhn's original observation that revolutionary scientists are more creative, Maslow has added more mature, more patient, tolerant, intuitive, understanding, and profound than are normal scientists. They are also generally better, freer, more devoted, and even more adept when it comes to the wheelhouse of the normal scientist than are the normal scientists.

Maslow is not alone in his efforts at lambasting the prevailing logical empirical scientific paradigms of twentieth century psychology. Qualitative methodologists William Braud and Rosemarie Anderson (1998) have described the dominant paradigms, that is, those research approaches that "model themselves after those of the physical sciences of the eighteenth and nineteenth centuries" (p. 5) in a similar manner:

> More important, such assumptions and practices yield a picture of the world, and of human nature and human possibility, that is narrow, constrained, fragmented, disenchanted, and deprived of meaning and value. Such a view is more consistent with feelings of emptiness, isolation, and alienation than with feelings of richness, interconnection, creativity, freedom, and optimism. (p. 6)

It is not merely that logical empirical programs are limited in scope, but that they are impoverished and inhumane. Furthermore, Braud et al find the proponents of modernist psychology to be "closed, authoritarian, competitive, absolute ('right answer'), elitist, individualistic, secretive, arcane, hierarchical, arrogant, alienated/alienating" (p. 12). For comparison, they describe an alternative psychology that in principle "[b]alances mechanistic/reductionistic, rational approaches with organismic, holistic, intuitive, experimental ones" as "humble" and "liberating" (p. 12).

In these unbecoming descriptions of the logical empirical practice of psychology, we find words that suggest that a practice which proceeds with a definite set of psychological assumptions—that is, a 'normal' science. For example, the behaviorists in principle deny the explanatory efficacy of consciousness. When such explanations that include consciousness are deemed "superstitious" and more reminiscent of "voodoo" than of science (Watson, 1930, p. 2), then behaviorists have constructed a hierarchy as to what counts for psychological knowledge. For this, behaviorist psychologists are being criticized for narrowness of scope. By expanding the scope of psychology— what Braud et al literally call the "expanded view" (p. 12)—one finds a 'revolutionary' psychology. Here there is an expansion of the types of questions that can be asked, tools that can be used, and explanations that can be given. 'Revolutionary' turns in scientific practice hope to correct the limitations imposed by 'normal' practices. Braud et al explain:

> To counter this prevailing conception of science and of research, a number of contemporary thinkers have offered complementary assumptions and practices to correct previous imbalances and provide a more complete view of science and research that can more adequately apprehend the complexity, breadth, and depth of our world and of humanity. (p. 6)

It seems that the intention here is to support a scientific practice that is always opening up onto new possibilities—correcting imbalances, providing a more complete view, and approaching ever-further depths. It is as if a scientific practice may remain forever 'revolutionary'—challenging its own assumptions and expanding its own horizons. Instead, the authors—who are contributing to an alternative methodologies textbook—have a narrow form of inquiry in mind. "The expanded approaches to research and disciplined inquiry that we present in this volume are especially suited to research topics involving human experiences that are *personal, subjective, significant,* and *relevant*" (p. 19). Like Watson (1930) in his description of behaviorist psychology that neglects Wundt's (1897) role of the subject, the methods described by Braud et al neglect Wundt's role of the object. By assigning a series of unbecoming adjectives to the "prevailing paradigm" (p. 12), it becomes clear that the authors have a similarly hierarchical science in mind. Given the narrowness of scope of what counts for "human" to humanistic psychologists, it seems that another revolution is afoot—one that has been termed "posthumanism" (Wolfe, 2009) in the humanities and "speculative realism" (Bryant, Srnicek, and Harman, 2011) in continental philosophy.

Now the humanistic psychologists are found occupying a definite ground of methodological practice—the very ground at which it has become common practice for humanists to sling mud. Perhaps the revolution has ended, and humanistic psychology is more representative of a 'normal' science. This would be the case if we choose option one in the introduction, but not if we choose option two.

## Maslow Limits Goldstein's Concept of "Self-actualization" to the Human

The final example that indicates Maslow's shift to cult practice concerns a key concept in the humanistic psychologist's lexicon: "self-actualization." Though popularized as the peak of Maslow's (1962) hierarchy, the term was introduced by a biologist by the name of Kurt Goldstein. Goldstein (1934/1995) finds that "an organism is governed by a tendency to actualize, as much as possible, its individual capacities, its 'nature,' in the world" (p. 162). From his description, self-actualization sounds like a synonym for *Natura naturans* or the becoming of nature that is not limited to any single entity within nature. Goldstein discusses the capacity inherent in all organisms toward being, regardless of the level of sophistication that this requires. He sees all organisms indiscriminately as being-towards-self-actualization. There is no good or bad; there is only becoming. The self that becomes is one's actualized self. How Goldstein's concept of self-actualization represents nonhuman (specifically biosemiotic) elements integral to humanistic psychology is covered in chapter 4. Consider Goldstein's conception to the manner by which Maslow (1971/1976) has taken it up.

Maslow discusses Goldstein's biological analysis with an added element of will or intention—it is as though the organism is agentively seeking its balance. For example, he writes:

> A damaged organism isn't satisfied just to be what it is, merely damaged. It strives, presses, and pushes; it fights and struggles with itself in order to make itself into a unity again. From being a Unity, minus a lost capacity, it presses toward becoming a new kind of Unity in which the lost capacity no longer destroys its Unity. It governs itself, makes itself, re-creates itself. It is certainly active and not passive. (Maslow, 1971/1976, p. 115)

Fritz Perls had been a medical intern of Goldstein's, and the latter proved to be a powerful influence on the former. The self-actualization of which Perls speaks is decidedly different than that of Maslow's hierarchy. Perls (1969/1972) explains the variety of shapes that this process takes:

> A living organism is an organism, which consists of thousands and thousands of processes that require interchange with other media outside the boundary of the organism. There are processes here in the ashtray, too. There are electronic processes, atomic processes, but for our purpose, these processes are not visible, not relevant to its existence for us here. But in a living organism, the ego boundary has to be negotiated by us because there is something outside that is needed. There is food outside: I want this food; I want to make it mine, like me. So, I have to like this food. If I don't like it, if it is unlike me, I wouldn't touch it, I leave it outside the boundary. So something has to happen to get through the boundary and this is what we call contact. We touch, we get in contact, we stretch our boundary out to the thing in question. If we are rigid and can't move, then it remains there. When we live, we spend energies, we need energies to maintain this machine. (pp. 14-15)

Perls observes that one could just as easily discuss the self-actualization of an ash-tray as one might discuss the self-actualization of a single mother: neither one is of the self-initiated, autonomous sort. A flower will open and follow the path of the sun just as I will seek relief when my bladder is full; self-actualization adequately describes each scenario.

Dogmatic humanistic psychologists would not allow this comparison. Exemplified by Maslow, they have drawn a line of demarcation between "whole organisms" that actualize, and the rest of the cosmos, which follows the laws of Newtonian mechanics. That a line has been drawn is not at issue: lines help demarcate scientific subject-matter so that armchairs, medicine balls, and chandeliers do not overcrowd the humanistic psychologist's laboratory. But the humanistic psychologists have drawn this line *a priori*, deciding in advance what counts for human. The discussion of Problem Three will demonstrate the problems that follow from this premature decision. It comes from the intersection between the fields of cyber-technology and psychology. The discussion considers the line that has become increasingly blurred between technology and the humans that use it. Given their principled defense of the a priori human, humanists are loathe to accept that humans have begun to experience feelings of empathy, affection, and compassion—that is, uniquely human emotions—that are elicited by robots and computer programs. Rather than expand her definition of "human," Sherry Turkle (2012) maintains the humanist distinction between human and robot by negating subjective experience, explaining that the subject who feels cared for by her pet-robot has been duped into an "as if" feeling of concern.

As a cult, humanistic psychology indicates the assumption that each of the above paths might be taken. That is, its practice of psychology can be both open to possibility but limited in scope. This includes a belief that a particular philosophical tradition—mid-century continental philosophy—not only provides insight into psychological inquiry, but adequately includes the breadth and depth of psychological scope. Psychological phenomena that fall outside of this scope are dismissed as non psychological or some type of imposter. Attention paid to these phenomena is misplaced and/or dehumanizing. Practitioners of humanist science have two options: admit to a limited scope and promote an awareness of alternative approaches that investigate that which falls outside said scope. That is, take up an identity as Kuhn's (1962/2012) 'normal' science, which identifies itself positively by demonstrating what insights it can offer, and no longer negatively as that which it hopes to avoid. Humanist scientists might instead choose to remain open to the possibilities that have been shut down by traditional modernist and humanist conceptions of Nature, and continue to open up to revolutionary methodologies and evolving subject-matters. In both cases, the cult-status would evaporate. In the first instance, it would be acknowledged that humanist science promotes certain conceptions of Nature and denies others; its validity would be found not in its iron-clad mid-century ontological defense, but in the value of its scientific findings to the community. In the second instance, the continuously evolving foundations and shifting subject-matter would make dogmatic adherence to notions of humanity or methodological procedure unthinkable; its validity would be found in the defense provided by the still-evolving continental philosophies of science, and its value would be in providing and application of these theoretical developments. At present, this might look like an object-oriented psychology (Harman, 2002/2006, 2005).

*Chapter Two*

# The Problem with Nature's Division

The twentieth century task of psychology is wearing thin. The dissatisfaction had with mainstream psychological methods—methods that emphasize psychological fact over the understanding of persons—are well known among humanistic psychologists and ecopsychologists. Because of this singular focus, psychology is currently in danger of being dissolved as a twenty-first century academic discipline. Today it is only in the margins that one can find a conception of psychology that does not reduce the latter to bio- and neurological processes—however complex. If it cannot transform to meet the demands of a rapidly transforming world, it will cease to exist as an autonomous discipline and will instead be absorbed into the disciplines of biology and cognitive science. Whatever remains on the margins will be sorted into the disciplines of education, philosophy, and religious studies. I maintain that humanistic psychology and ecopsychology cannot be easily dissolved without losing something uniquely significant.

This past decade the humanities were facing a similar crisis that has important implications for humanistic psychology and ecopsychology. The president of the Dutch Consortium of European Sciences concluded that the humanities disciplines had repeatedly failed to evolve beyond anthropomorphic and anthropocentric studies (Braidotti, 2013). These perspectives maintain that the world can only be known insofar as it matters to humans. Anthropocentrism is the twofold assumption that humankind sits atop a hierarchy of living and nonliving things within the universe, and that living and nonliving things are meaningful only insofar as they matter to humankind. Anthropomorphism is the assumption that the essences of living and nonliving things have the likeness of, and are in principle understandable to humankind. Since the humanities include such disciplines as creative writing, rhetoric, literature, cultural studies, foreign languages, creative arts, and philosophy, among others, it is easy to see how the human perspective is integral to each. Indeed, each of these disciplines could be seen revolving around Da-Vinci's Vitruvian Man. By accusing the humanities disciplines of anthropocentrism and anthropomorphism, it was being argued that these disciplines have failed to investigate the role the environment plays in shaping culture, or even in attempting to understand the role the environment plays in noncultural ways—that is, in understanding the world before or after humans. In which ways has geography dictated cultural customs or rites of passage—thus geographizing regional civilizations? Music and art need not belong to the consciousness of the musicians and artists, but could be understood as responses to and in the language of changing seasons. The humanities have responded in impressive fashion, including an entire book-series devoted to the posthuman (Posthumanities: University of Minnesota Press).

While it is an important detail for humanistic psychology to recognize and address, anthropocentrism is particularly important for ecopsychology. Anthropocentrism undermines the entire project of ecopsychology by perpetuating the very dissociation from and alienation to nature that it warns against. Furthermore, the consequences of an anthropocentric ecopsychology are shared by humans and nature.

## ANTHROPOCENTRISM AND THE HUMAN-NATURE DIVIDE IN ECOPSYCHOLOGY

The growth of psychology as a twentieth century discipline saw many decades of the machine metaphor for behavior and thinking. From associationism in bio-psychology to behaviorism in learning theory to information processing in cognition, the human has been understood as a machine in a remarkably vast number of ways. Humanistic psychologists stood out among psychological subdivisions as being *opposed* to the mechanization of the human, and with good reason. Indeed, the processes of being human *are* far too complicated and subtle to be summarized by the predictable coordination of discrete and separate parts. The problem with this distinction was that many humanistic psychologists were inclined to draw a line of demarcation between humans and the rest of nature. Maslow (1966) demonstrates this when he writes that "while it was necessary and helpful to dehumanize planets, rocks, and animals, we are realizing more and more strongly that it is *not* necessary to dehumanize the human being and to deny him human purposes" (p. 2). Maslow argues against the mechanization of the human on the grounds that humans are not like other entities found in nature like planets, rocks, and animals. He implies that we may continue to reduce these to machines, but that humans deserve special attention.

Maslow is correct in decrying the mechanization of the human, but he stops too soon! Biologists, chemists, botanists, entomologists, and even physicists have also been arguing against the continued mechanization of their subject matter (Simeonov, Rosen, and Gare, 2015; Emmeche and Kull, 2011; Hoffmeyer, 2008; Cobb and Griffin, 1977). By arguing for the unique treatment of the human category, Maslow effectively draws a line in-between humans and nature. Furthermore, he ranks the former above the latter.

When Maslow differentiates humans from the rest of nature, he introduces a category of separateness. Humans are in one category and they are to be humanized. The rest of nature may be put into a second category to be mechanized—*de*humanized, as it were. With this line of separation, it is understood that humans are separate from nature. By suggesting that they deserve special treatment, Maslow also implies that humans are situated above nature as though they are superior to it.

The *de facto* separation of humans from the rest of nature may be understood as carry-over from previous, theological worldviews of humankind. Humans were understood to be created in the image of God—the latter an anthropomorphized deity. Being children of God (presupposed or not) has its privileges: the flora and fauna of the world must capitulate to the will of humankind. As Medieval theology is supplanted by modern scientific thinking, humankind still occupies a position of centrality in the universe as the geocentric model of the solar system maintains. The God-given privilege carries over even in the absence of God as humans assume a central place in the universe. And once again when the geocentric model is supplanted with the heliocentric model, the privilege of the centrality of humankind in the universe remains: post enlightenment humans are now free to exert control over anything they so choose. It is their God-given, er—"natural" right.

Despite growing evidence to the contrary, the assumption that humans occupy some central place of importance and privilege in the universe has been carried over from previous worldviews. It is found quite explicitly in the earlier works of French phenomenologist Maurice Merleau-Ponty (1942/1963). Merleau-Ponty describes three orders of nature (human, vital, physical) that vary in terms of integration and complexity. The human order that has been blessed with consciousness and mind, the vital order that demonstrates a sort of mindless complexity and dynamism, and finally the physical order of objects that bounce off of one another. However, as he differentiates between these three orders it becomes clear that his only reason for their separation is the carried-over expectation that the be separated. In no way does Merleau-Ponty give the indication that the separation of orders is helpful or even insightful. It thus comes as no surprise that he would later discard his divisions in favor of a flattened ontology of *flesh* (1964/1968). Humanistic psychology does not need to re-think its conception of the human-nature relationship. Indeed, it needs only to let go of the carried-over assumption that humans must be separate from the rest of nature, and may follow Merleau-Ponty's lead in doing so.

## DIVIDING HUMANS FROM NATURE: MERLEAU-PONTY'S HIERARCHICAL CATEGORIZATION OF NATURE

This section examines Merleau-Ponty's (1942/1963) division of nature into mutually exclusive orders of life. This is important in the present volume because Merleau-Ponty has become an important philosopher among humanistic psychologists. His phenomenology has supported a broad variety of methods of research and practice, and is relied upon heavily by the human science research movement. If Merleau-Ponty has argued for a division between humankind and nature, then it suggests that any subsequent research that has benefited from his ontology is doomed to anthropocentrism. However, Merleau-Ponty has also been used to argue against this customary division of nature. In his unfinished notes (posthumously published as *Visible and the Invisible*, 1964/1968), Merleau-Ponty introduces his ontology of *flesh*—something in which humans and nonhumans alike participate. It is argued that Merleau-Ponty's division of nature into distinct orders *actually does more to emphasize similarities than differences*, which makes the ontology developed in *Structure* no less radical than that developed in *Visible and the Invisible*. Moreover, this ontology promotes interdisciplinary research. In the analysis, arguments for and against the division of nature into mutually exclusive orders are supported by biologists (Goldstein, 1934/1995; Pantin, 1968; Leclerc, 1977), physicists (Schrödinger, 1944/1967), psychologists (Rosen, 2008), and philosophers (Mazis, 2008; Hartshorne, 1977; Thorpe, 1977) over the last several decades. In sum, the exemplar of humanistic science has never supported a division between humankind and nature.

In his first academic monograph, *Structure of Behavior,* Merleau-Ponty integrates a great deal of exciting research across the physical, biological, and psychological sciences. These are domains of scientific interest that would continue to inform his scholarship. With it he delivers an impressive blow to the application of mechanical models to the human, which had become popular at that time. For example, Merleau-Ponty borrows from Goldstein's (1934/1995) holistic biological analysis of the human as well as Köhler's (1947/1957) work with perception in humans and animals. The result of this integration is a proposal for an amendment to psychological and biological sciences. The subsequent completion of *Phenomenology of Perception* (1945/1962) demonstrates the direction that Merleau-Ponty goes following this systematic critique of the philosophy of mechanism in the sciences. In this regard, *Structure* may be read as a prequel to *Phenomenology of Perception.*

This latter point poses some problems for the recent popularity with the use of Merleau-Ponty's approach for understanding posthuman subjectivity (e.g., Mazis, 2008; Rosen, 2008, Harman, 2005; and Abram, 1996)—positions that this present work is in favor of. Indeed, it suggests that these positions are untenable! However, as flesh, Merleau-Ponty later argues that nature is an undivided fabric. As such, it seems as though a non-anthropocentric phenomenology might be possible. In order to defend a non-anthropocentric phenomenology—that is, a phenomenology that does not begin and end with a particular socio-historical human—Merleau-Ponty's later work concerning nature as flesh will have to be distinguished from his earlier proposal in *Structure*. Conceived as flesh, nature may be understood as a single and undivided fabric; according to *Structure of Behavior*, it seems that nature may be divided into three distinct orders. These are the orders of the physical, vital, and human (1942/1963, pp. 129-184).

## THE ORDERS OF NATURE OUTLINED IN MERLEAU-PONTY'S *STRUCTURE OF BEHAVIOR*

With Merleau-Ponty (1942/1963), we find a stepwise progression in structural integration and capacity. He reasons that physical entities, vital entities, and human entities must necessarily participate unequally in nature. That is, these entities may be discerned by their range of capabilities and limitations. Moreover, these inequities constitute a hierarchy of individuality. By "individuality," it is understood that the entity in question is not divisible, but that it is an integrated and unchanging whole. Theoretical physicist and phenomenological philosopher Steven Rosen (2008) reminds us that "The Greek word 'atom' is functionally equivalent to the word 'individual': both mean 'not divisible'" (p. 9). Individuality is not an anthropomorphic term, but a term that relates to indivisibility in elemental matter.

Also in fidelity to any proposed hierarchical division of orders within nature, it must be noted that there are no boundary entities. This is to say that there may be no entities that straddle the boundary between two of the orders (e.g., the physical and the vital). Any entity that resembles two orders separately would undermine the rules of order placement. For example, entities in the vital order are in this order specifically because they have something (integrity, capacity) that entities in the lower physical order in principle do not. Merleau-Ponty (1942/1963) explains how "[b]y definition, it would be impossible to conceive of a physical form which had the same properties as a physiological form and a physiological form which was the equivalent of a mental form" (p. 133).

To repeat: It may be understood that Merleau-Ponty proposes three distinct orders of nature that are mutually exclusive and hierarchically related. It may also be understood that these orders are jointly exhaustive though it is never explicitly stated. What follows is a close analysis of this claim. A case is made for discerning human entities from physical entities (Hartshorne, 1977), and a case is made for discerning vital entities from physical entities (Thorpe, 1977; Schrödinger, 1944/1967).

## The Argument that Human Entities Are Distinct from Physical Entities

Merleau-Ponty is not alone in his conviction that entities in nature participate unequally. Indeed, one need not return to the nineteenth century to find compelling support for these divisions. Hartshorne (1977) provides a list of "reasons for thinking that inanimate objects such as rocks and chairs are devoid of mind" (p. 91). That is, there are distinct reasons why the physical may be distinguished from the human. He provides the following list:

1. Their inertness, inactivity, motionlessness. They do not seem to do anything.
2. Their lack of freedom in the sense of initiative, creative departure from mere routine. The predictability of astronomical events is a good example. The sole motions seem wholly matters of routine, or statistical upshots of huge members of microevents, as in the sun's corona.
3. Their lack of individuality in the sense of unity and uniqueness. If a chair has parts—pieces of wood, metal, plastic, etc—why assign feeling or memory, say, to the whole chair rather than to each piece of wood, each nail or screw? In non-living things visible to the naked eye there is no clear distinction between whole and part, and no dynamic unity, as though something like a sequence of experiences were influencing those parts.
4. Their lack of apparent intrinsic purpose. (Hartshorne, 1977, p. 91)

Merleau-Ponty differentiates between the orders of nature by emphasizing greater or lesser structural integration, individuality, and capacity. To this list, Hartshorne has added four new distinctions between physical entities and human entities. "Higher order" will refer to objects with mind while "lower order" for those without. He explains that higher order entities are active while the lower, inactive; higher order entities demonstrate initiative while the lower, routine; lower orders are capable of being anonymously swept up into a gestalt whole, while the higher orders are not; and lower orders and the higher orders display intrinsic purpose while the lower lack any apparent intrinsic purpose. Like Merleau-Ponty, Hartshorne maintains that these factors determine the order to which a given entity belongs, and that these entities are hierarchical, mutually exclusive, and jointly exhaustive.

## The Argument that Vital Entities Are Distinct from Physical Entities

Hartshorne provides a way of distinguishing the entities of the physical order from the entities of the psychological order. Thorpe (1977) distinguishes the entities of the physiological order from those of the physical. He also provides four examples.

> So we can say: (a) What organisms *do* is different from what *happens* to stones. (b) The parts of organisms are functional and are inter-related one with another to form a system which is working in a particular way or appears to be designed for a particular direction of activity. In other words the system is directive, or if we like to use the word in a very wide and loose sense, 'purposive.' [... And (d)] that organisms absorb and store information, change their behavior as a result of that information, and all but the very lowest forms of animals (and perhaps these too) have special organs for detecting, sorting, and organizing this information—namely the sense organs and specialized parts of the central nervous system. (Thorpe, 1977, p. 3)

In distinguishing physical entities from vital entities, Thorpe provides three key points. Point (c) has been removed since it amounts to nothing more than a tautological statement of difference. This will be important in the subsequent part of the present section because it demonstrates the how these categories have been erected *de facto* with what seems like little attention to the entities therein. Thus, it is fitting that Thorpe's third distinction between physical entities and vital entities is that they're different. Thorpe's three points may be understood as characteristics found in vital entities that are lacking in physical entities. They are volition, purpose, and the ability to store information. It is worth noting that Schrödinger (1944/1967) has written a lovely volume titled *What is Life?* where he observes the profound differences between organic and inorganic entities. Organic matter—that is, living matter for Schrödinger—is reliably organized based on a single (and sometimes double) copy of deoxyribonucleic acid (DNA). He writes of this,

> Whether we find it astonishing or whether we find it quite plausible that a small but highly organized group of atoms be capable of acting in this manner, the situation is unprecedented, it is unknown anywhere else except living matter. The physicist and the chemist, investigating inanimate matter, have never witnessed phenomena which they had to interpret in this way. (p. 79)

Schrödinger's enthusiastic review of DNA follows a long description of the relative disorganization of nonliving matter. Indeed, the laws of nonliving matter apply only as aggregate probabilities. To give a substance a specific half-life says nothing of the probability of a single molecule of that substance maintaining potency indefinitely. Indeed, the behavior of a single molecule is entirely uncertain. However, with living matter, Schrödinger observes that single cells play a predictable role of organizing entire organisms. He notes how this is without precedent in the physical world.

In summary, Merleau-Ponty (1942/1963) has proposed the division of nature into three orders that are related in a hierarchy such that the higher entities exhibit individual integration and capacity that is denied the lower entities. Furthermore, these orders are mutually exclusive and jointly exhaustive. Hartshorne (1977) has provided four compelling points of difference between physical and human entities; the latter he has defined as objects with mind. Thorpe (1977) has provided three compelling points of difference between physical entities and vital entities, and Schrödinger (1944/1967), a fourth.

## NATURE RESISTS DIVISION: AMBIGUITY IN MERLEAU-PONTY'S DIVIDING LINES

Merleau-Ponty's (1942/1963) observation "that matter, life, and mind must participate unequally in nature" comes at the end of his critique of mechanization—that is, modernist models of explanation in physical (physics), vital (physiology), and human (psychology) sciences. Its placement at the end implies that this hierarchy is the logical conclusion to *Structure of Behavior*, and thus the logical starting point in *Phenomenology of Perception.* This is to say that the first constructive thing that might be said about moving forward after the systematic critique of mechanisticity is that three divisions still remain and that they share a hierarchical relationship. *Structure of Behavior* provides a cry against an exclusively mechanical understanding of all entities in science.

However, anybody reading Merleau-Ponty's *Structure* will notice that once he has dismissed the modernist ontology of mechanism, the traditionally separated orders share more similarities than differences! As such, his chapter on the separate orders of nature is ill-fitting! I argue that his segregation and hierarchization of nature is not a culminating argument of *Structure* as much as a *de facto* assertion of ontological and ethological differences across these three traditional orders. Instead of dividing it, Merleau-Ponty effectively flattens out the nineteenth century hierarchical division of nature that had been based on structural complexity and sophistication. *Once this has occurred, one finds that "life" is a characteristic across all three orders.* Yet he concludes his work by asserting that hierarchical differences still exist. In sum, the lines that Merleau-Ponty has used to divide nature do little to segregate the entities therein. After his systematic critique of mechanistic-ity in psychological and biological theory, Merleau-Ponty (1942/1963) argues against the utility of mechanical theories for *any* branch of science. He includes Köhler's critique of a mechanical model in human perception; he argues for Goldstein's non-mechanical model for organismic processes; and then he maintains that the mechanistic model is no longer appropriate for physical bodies either. He explains,

> The physical experiment is never the revelation of an isolated causal series: one verifies that the observed effect indeed obeys the presumed law by taking into account a series of conditions, such as temperature, atmospheric pressure, altitude, in brief, that is, a certain number of laws which are independent of those which constitute the proper object of the experiment. (p. 139)

This is to say that the "isolated variable" that is the focus of a physical experiment can never in principle be isolated from its physical milieu. In measuring barometric pressure, one is necessarily also measuring tempera-ture, altitude, humidity, etc. Merleau-Ponty is not alone in his conviction that mechanical models are no longer tenable for understanding the physical or-der. Thorpe (1977) observes the change in the conception of atoms from classical to contemporary physics when he writes,

> Atoms were thought to be permanent, unchanging elements of nature. Now, far from remaining unaltered, they appear to be created, destroyed, and trans-muted. What do remain enduring are certain abstract attributes of particles, of which the electric charge and the wave aspects of elementary physical particles are most familiar. (p. 1)

When Hartshorne (1977) distinguishes physical entities from human ones, he notes that the former are guided by routine and the latter, freedom. What Thorpe notices seems to be at odds with this. Rather than being guided by routine, physical particles seem to be recalcitrant to routine. "At bottom all the quantum principles assert that there are no devices by which we can wholly control what state of a system we will observe next" (Thorpe, 1977, p. 1).

## Complexity Marks the Shift from Classical to Contemporary Thinking

At the beginning of the twentieth century, classical models of physics had become increasingly untenable. Whitehead (1920/2012) recounts the shift as it had been caught by the popular presses:

> [D]uring the last few weeks the scientific journals and the lay press have been filled with articles as to the nature of the crucial experiments which have been

made and as to some of the more striking expressions of the outcome of the
new theory. 'Space caught bending' appeared on the news-sheet of a well-
known evening paper.... (Whitehead, 1920/2012, p. 85)

Such lay and scientific journal attention was due to a series of shocking
experiments that drew the classical conception of physical reality into question. Rosen (2008) provides additional commentary to one such shocking
experiment, and indicates how it drew the classical physical model into question:

> When Michelson and Morley measured the velocity of light from different
> frames of reference, instead of encountering the differences that they and
> every other researcher had fully expected, light's velocity remained the same.
> In the perceptual analogy, it would be as if the objects on my desk would look
> exactly the same to me regardless of my angle of view. Michelson and Mor-
> ley's strange discovery was most alarming to physicists. In fact it was a bomb-
> shell that was soon to precipitate the Einsteinian revolution. That is because
> the finding of Michelson and Morley did nothing less than call into question
> the classical intuition of object-in-space-before-subject that had implicitly
> governed human experience for many centuries. (p. 163)

The last point that Rosen makes is important in understanding the unclarity
of nature's dividing lines, and it will also prove consequential for the remainder of the present chapter. In the classical model, as Rosen observes, there is
the ontological assumption that objects participate in human events in a
passive and mechanical fashion. The Michelson/Morley experiment suggests
a collapse of this passive interaction and a dynamic intertwining of subject
and object. Leclerc (1977) will be used to consider this further, below.

Merleau-Ponty (1942/1963) also makes an important point that the modernist model of mechanical-objective realism is no longer sufficient as an
exclusive model for understanding entities in nature. This goes for barstools
and bonobos. Once again, it is at *this* point that he has inserted a section
reminding his readers that even though the categories of physical, vital, and
human share the attribute of complexity, they might still be kept separate.
Even though it has been established that all of nature demonstrates high
levels of complexity, activity, and dynamism, Merleau-Ponty has nevertheless asserted a *de facto* separation between these orders of nature. Leclerc
(1977) has called this the tendency to "carry over" classical physical conceptions into contemporary conceptions—and this even occurs when the latter
have been used to critique the former! In order to understand how Merleau-
Ponty might reintroduce outdated systems of division, a moment will be
taken to distinguish the classical conceptions of the physical order from the
contemporary amendments to these (demonstrated by Merleau-Ponty's critique of mechanism across each of his orders of nature). That is, despite his

critique of mechanical-objective realism, Merleau-Ponty still maintains (or "carries over") some of the consequences of this model of explanation. This is how he is able to assert a *de facto* division of nature into three mutually exclusive orders.

In characterizing the time during which Merleau-Ponty and Whitehead had been writing, Leclerc notes how "the last hundred years and more has rendered unacceptable the conception of the physical which had dominated scientific thought since the seventeenth century" (p. 101). In the classical conception of nature, lifeless matter could be distinguished from living matter in terms of activity. Leclerc (1977) writes,

> The only change possible in respect of the physical as 'matter' was purely external change of place, i.e., of *being moved* from one place to another.
>
> But the result of the development of science has been that in this century there has occurred a *de facto* abandonment of that early modern conception of the physical. It is now on the whole implicitly or explicitly accepted in the basic sciences that physical existents are somehow and in some respect 'alive.' (p. 101)

With the exception of Schrödinger's (1944/1967) observations about the highly predictable ordering of living (organic) matter, which physical matter lacks, Leclerc (1977) collapses the distinction between physical and vital. The difference between animate and inanimate entities—that is, physiological and physical entities—may no longer be determined by the living-lifeless distinction. There is no lifeless matter, only matter in the process of becoming.

At this juncture it is important to note how the differences between the physical and vital orders of nature are less clear than a sharp line of demarcation allows. The shift from classical (mechanisticity) to contemporary (complexity/sophisticated realism) has been marked by a recognition of similarities across the classical lines of nature's division. However, Leclerc and Rosen have observed that "carry-over" of classical consequences has occurred. Despite a necessary shift in the conception of nature, some of the consequences of the now untenable conception of nature (classical) have continued into the new conception (contemporary). Merleau-Ponty's (1942/1963) *de facto* separation of nature into three orders has been implicated as an example of this. When this *de facto* separation is considered in more detail, even Merleau-Ponty himself observes that there are more similarities across these divisions than there are differences

## Merleau-Ponty's Divisions in Detail: Emphasizing Similarities over Differences

It will again be stressed that Merleau-Ponty has begun his discussion concerning the orders of nature with the recognition that each of these orders represent a complexity that far exceeds that by which they have traditionally been understood through classical (i.e., modern) models. Merleau-Ponty discusses each of these orders—physical, vital, and human—in turn. Since references will be made to his text, Merleau-Ponty's terminology will be used.

### Physical – Vital

Merleau-Ponty maintains that while neither physical bodies nor organic bodies may be understood as operating under the mechanical laws of modern physics, one must necessarily still observe differences between them. However, it is difficult to understand where the key difference emerges. For example, Merleau-Ponty (1942/1963) recognizes the similarities between the vital and physical orders:

> Often, the quantitative relations with which physics is concerned are only the formulae for certain distributive processes: in a soap bubble as in an organism, what happens at each point is determined by what happens at all the others. But this is the definition of Order.
>
> There is therefore no reason whatsoever for refusing objective value to this category in the study of the phenomena of life, since it has its place in the definition of physical systems. (p. 131)

The physical and vital orders both operate, at least in part, in an orderly manner. Moreover, neither operates by the simple unidirectional arrow of causality the way the classical physicists had assumed, but are instead embedded within a web of relations. Both are more or less ordered, and each is contingent upon the surrounding environment of relations. How then might they be distinguished? Merleau-Ponty argues that the locus of order is what differentiates the physiological from the physical. The order of physical matter is determined from without; the order of living matter is determined from within:

> Doubtless certain physical systems modify the very conditions upon which they depend by their internal evolution.... But action which is exercised outside the system always has the effect of reducing a state of tension, of advancing the system toward rest. We speak of [physiological] entities, on the contrary, when equilibrium is obtained, not with respect to real and present conditions, but with respect to conditions which are only virtual and which the system itself brings into existence; when the entity, instead of procuring a release from the forces with which it is penetrated through the pressure of

external ones, executes a work beyond its proper limits and constitutes a proper milieu for itself. (pp. 145-146)

Once again, Merleau-Ponty allows for the possibility that a physical body might regulate itself. Yet this is followed by an argument that the same body is still contingent on its environment. The physiological entity, it seems, differs from the physical in that it has the capacity of shaping its own milieu. It might be added here that the physiological entity that affects a change on its environment has done so without compromising its own integrity. Otherwise it might be argued that an oxygen-atom might exercise its vitality by requisitioning the valence electrons of another oxygen-atom. Another way of stating this difference is that the physical entity is acted upon by the world whereas for the vital entity, the world is acted upon.

> One cannot assign a moment in which the world acts on the organism, since the very effect of this "action" expresses the internal law of the organism. The mutual exteriority of the organism and the milieu is surmounted along with the mutual exteriority of the stimuli. (p. 161)

Referring again to the oxygen atom from the previous example—as a vital entity, the atom's exteriority surmounts the exteriority of its fellow oxygen atom in the creation of an oxygen molecule with a mutual exteriority. The now-surmounted oxygen atom, representing a physical entity, has been acted upon. In either case, it seems as though individual initiative may be attributed after the fact of an interaction to whichever entity remains the least changed.

In summary, Merleau-Ponty maintains that the vital order is, indeed, distinct from the physical. While they bear much in common like order, non-linear causation, and embeddedness in their surround, vital entities are organized from within while physical entities are organized from without. This may also be stated in terms of action and inaction: physiological entities act upon their surround while physical entities are acted upon. While Merleau-Ponty has acknowledged an integral difference between the physical and physiological orders, this has been accompanied by a range of similarities. It will be the purpose of the latter part of the paper to examine the possible collapse of this line of demarcation.

## Vital – Human

Merleau-Ponty has discerned the physical order from the vital order by arguing that the latter is itself responsible for its order whereas the former is not, and that vital entities are able to effect change on their environment whereas the physical entities are affected. Next he distinguishes the human order from the vital order. Merleau-Ponty is very clear about this difference. "Man can never be an animal: his life is always more or less integrated than that of an animal" (p. 181). But he follows this up with a qualifying statement that fudges the edges of the clear differentiation he just provided. "But if the alleged instincts of man do not exist apart from the mental dialectic, correlatively, this dialectic is not conceivable outside of the concrete situations in which it is embodied" (p. 181). This represents a very interesting inner dialogue between what might be understood as the author of *Phenomenology of Perception* (1942/1962) and that of *The Visible and the Invisible* (1964/1968). The former is, of course, interested in understanding the uniquely human act of perception; the latter is interested in collapsing this uniqueness into the world of flesh. He first asserts the facticity of the division between vital and human orders, but then gives an example of how even reflex actions represent an interactive engagement with the environment—an observation he has borrowed from Kurt Goldstein (1934/1995). It is almost as if Merleau-Ponty feels like he must defend the anthropocentric uniqueness of the human order, whereas his intuition is that there really is no reason to suppose that humans are more integrated than animals.

Merleau-Ponty argues that the human order is distinct from the vital order by magnitude of integration. Moreover, both remain distinct from the physical order in their capacity to act upon their surroundings. The human entities do so with an integrated mind. This provides the first key distinction between human and physiological. Human entities are capable of creating curiously Marxist objects with commodity-value that exceed their use-value. Human entities build cities, wear articles of clothing, and design living room interiors whereas vital entities experience object-fixedness:

> A nest is an object which has a meaning only in relation to the possible behavior of the organic individual; if a monkey picks a branch in order to reach a goal, it is because it is able to confer a functional value on an object of nature. But monkeys scarcely succeed at all in constructing instruments which would serve only for preparing others; we have seen that, having become a stick for a monkey, the tree branch is eliminated as such—which is the equivalent of saying that it is never possessed as an instrument in the full sense of the word. (Merleau-Ponty, p. 175)

Merleau-Ponty concedes that both humans and animals may be found constructing tools. The former are capable of constructing them for no other purpose than constructing more (sophisticated) tools, an ability that animals do not share. Though this seems to have been contradicted by Köhler's (1947/1957) commentary to his work on insight-based problem solving. Merleau-Ponty has carried over the idea that humanness is more complicated than animalness, and has ignored the insights of the gestaltists of whom he was a great fan! He distinguishies humans from animals in terms of total integration, and in the former's capacity for first- *and* second-order meaning of objects. Vital entities are limited to the first-order meaning—that is, an object as it is currently being used. While Köhler's chimpanzees have combined two poles of insufficient length together to create a pole that reaches bananas, Merleau-Ponty reasons that the identity of these poles will now be limited to "banana-reaching poles" and no longer used for jousting or high-jumping.

Merleau-Ponty also makes the case that humans possess a consciousness that animals do not have. He uses the child's acquisition of language as an example. Like Noam Chomsky would eventually famously argue, Merleau-Ponty explains how a child's acquisition of a language cannot possibly be described by operant conditioning: no amount of reinforcement in the environment could condition something as complicated as French. He argues that children are "pre-figured" to grasp meaning in spoken word. This, of course, is because humans are conscious. He writes that "If language did not encounter some predisposition for the act of speech in the child who hears speaking, it would remain for him a sonorous phenomenon among others for a long time" (p. 169).

While animals—as in Goldstein's *The Organism*—are capable of meaningful transformation within a milieu, this plasticity is not sufficient in understanding the acquisition of a language. Indeed, it would take eons for a child to engage each novel sound, integrating them into his or her milieu until every available sound and combination of sounds had been mastered. Merleau-Ponty observes that even the recognition of the type of sound harkens a specific sort of awareness. Though juxtaposition with the communication between animals has not been provided, it may be understood by extension that theirs lacks the element of consciousness. Otherwise it could be argued that human voices would not sound sonorous to wolverines either, and wolverine pups would also acquire the French language with shocking rapidity. This is, of course, a straw man argument. The only reason for blaming the acquisition of French on the sophistication of consciousness and the acquisition of wolverine language on conditioning is based only on the assumption that humans have something animals do not. It is another instance of carry-over of the classical and even theological divisions in nature.

Finally, Merleau-Ponty describes the tendency for perception to occur as an entire gestalt event. His example is the sense you get about its inhabitants upon walking into an apartment. An apartment delivers a physiognomy in perception; it presents with it a character of distinct singularity. This character is not to be understood as the rational sum of visible, auditory, and olfactory parts. Instead, these components combine into the single apartment with which psychological entities interact and by which they're changed. With this example, Merleau-Ponty once again neglects to juxtapose the human with the animal, so it is uncertain whether this gestalt experience is unique to humans or extends to animals as well. In either case, Merleau-Ponty provides an example of how the components of an apartment might combine to present as a unity. These apparently individual parts of a setting come together in their interaction with humans. That is, one does not find an integrated being on one side and a pile of inert objects on the other, but an event of integrated beings.

The strength of Merleau-Ponty's argument that humans belong to an order that is distinct from animals comes only from the a priori assumption that this is the case. None of his examples prove satisfactory. Indeed, had he given them the kind of attention and patience that is the hallmark of his *Phenomenology*, then he would certainly have concluded otherwise or at least suspended judgment. The power of carry-over is considerable.

Aside from the carried-over assumption that nature be divided, it seems that these orders share more similarities than differences. In terms of their similarities, the following section will provide evidence for a more graduated distribution of nature. That is, rather than arguing for mutual exclusivity, a few key characteristics might be traced across the whole range of orders. The following section provides evidence for life across all of nature's orders.

## Nature's Division as a Graduated Continuum with Life at Each Order

It has already been seen that Merleau-Ponty has had great difficulty maintaining mutual exclusivity between his orders of nature. Once again, the proposal that these orders be mutually exclusive entails that one cannot expect to find a vital entity to demonstrate the individual integration or capacity that marks a human entity, etc. While there might be a range of entities that satisfy the specifications within each order, there is a definite gap in individual integration and capacity between each order. *As such, we may drop the attribute of mutual exclusivity when speaking of orders within nature.* This move changes two things: first, it does not restrict a given entity to a specific order; and second, it implies that the defining characteristics of each order (e.g., individual integration) may be found in any entity. The first change suggests that an entity is not limited to any one order, but may pass between them based on temporal integration and capacity. That is, the orders still differentiate between entities in terms of integration and capacity, but a given entity may demonstrate much integration at one moment and very little at another. The second change is a corollary to the first: if any entity could pass from one order to the next and back again, then the defining characteristics of each order must be evident in each of the entities that comprise nature. Together, these changes may be understood as a flexibility of dividing boundaries as well as a flexibility of structural individualities within nature. For example, an atom, insofar as it demonstrates high levels of individual integration and capacity, may be found within the human order; a human, insofar as it demonstrates low levels of individual integration and capacity, may be found in the physical order; and so on.

Merleau-Ponty (1964/1968) demonstrates how this antinomy might unfold within a single person with his demonstration of left-hand-touching right-hand-touching-things. Here's how it works: touch something with your right hand—it can be this book, your shirt collar, or the chair that you're sitting on. Notice how your right hand acts as a sense-vehicle of the object it is investigating. Gone to you is the sensation along your back of the chair you occupy; your awareness is through your right hand. The fabric of your shirt collar or the upholstery of your chair do not touch your right hand, but the reverse. As you are exploring the world through your right hand, reach over with the left and touch your right hand. If you can, indeed, feel your right hand with your left fingers, then the former will feel inert and lifeless (even though it is still in contact with whichever object it had been investigating). This relationship can reverse in a moment so that your left fingertips can feel can feel like lifeless prongs on the backside of your right hand. In this example, the right hand goes from a human hand capable of sensory exploration (Merleau-Ponty even speaks of multiple consciousnesses for each sensing finger) to an inert object, stubborn to the will of another, and back again to the vehicle for sense awareness. In but a few moments we see the human hand shift from the human order to the physical order and back again.

Entities in nature may pass freely between the orders. The passage from one to another indicates that their relationship with their surrounding environment has changed. As vehicles for communicating sense-awareness of the environment, hands may be understood either biosemiotically or psychologically. And as an object of sensory properties available for exploration by a sensing entity, hands may be understood physically. Merleau-Ponty's 'hands' example gives us an example of how entities within the human order may pass into the vital or physical orders. So too might we understand that entities within the physical order may pass freely into other orders as well. Consider an assortment of mundane objects or particles—e.g., the pile of books that sits beside me. Though apparently inert and lifeless, the argument is that even these books are composed of living processes, and as such their relationship to the environment and to one another has the potential to change rather markedly. That they merely stand by passively for the gaze of subjects is a powerful assumption that has survived the shift from classical to contemporary science that Rosen (2008) and Leclerc (1977) have described. In a chapter of a volume titled *Mind in Nature* (Cobb and Griffin, 1977), Hartshorne would maintain that these books are not only active, but are even capable of demonstrating initiative:

> Macroscopic inanimate objects are now known to be not the unitary, simply solid, inactive things they appear to be, but rather collections of numerous

distinct, highly active things (molecules, atoms, particles). And there is no
evidence that such things are wholly devoid of initiative; what evidence there
is suggests the opposite. (p. 91)

That Hartshorne is willing to attribute volitional capacity to inanimate objects should come as no surprise given his Whiteheadian panpsychic conception of nature. He recognizes that even the most inactive, inert, and lifeless
entities are made up of highly active things. While it is a bit of a stretch to
conflate activity with life, the recognition of complexity and activity within
all matter is important in understanding the shift from classical to contemporary thought. Before fusing the inanimate physical entities together with the
living, human entities, consider first the similarities across physical and vital
entities.

While activity at the level of inanimate physical entities is an improvement, it is still found within the discourse of classical physical matter. I can
push on the side of this growing pile of books such that the tower begins to
collapse. For a little more than a second, the book-pile is active—that is, it is
undergoing a locomotive change. The new book-pile no longer resembles a
tower and thus becomes a new entity. Indeed, even the physical interrelationships between books have now changed. Yet each of these descriptions of
change remain on the level of the classical paradigm—the book system parts
exist separately in-themselves and only their physical relationships change. *If
one were to instead propose that the fallen tower's new identity also changed
the identity of its constitutive books, then there would be a departure from the
classic paradigm.* Leclerc (1977) calls this the "conception of the physical as
in a 'process of becoming.'" With this he moves from the inorganic physical
sciences and into the organic biological sciences by emphasizing the similarity of constituent parts—physics has its atoms, electrons, and protons; chem-
istry has its atoms and molecules; biology has its cells, organs, and organ-
systems. What is emphasized in each of these sciences is the character of
interrelatedness between the constituents of each entity.

From Igor Leclerc we learn that the orders of nature may be understood as
a gradual distribution—that is, life is exhibited in each order though in increasing complexity. This is distinct from Merleau-Ponty's mutually exclusive orders for the fact that there is no single attribute that separates one order
from another. Instead, orders may be understood in terms of varying degrees
of life. Leclerc supplies an alternative to Merleau-Ponty's mutually exclusive
orders while still allowing for varying degrees of sophistication, life, mentality, etc. And indeed, after reviewing the sum total of Merleau-Ponty's ontology, he would certainly lean more toward Leclerc's conception.

In addition to more appropriately modeling a post-classical conception of
nature, this model solves philosophical and scientific problems as well. Sof-
tening the ontological boundaries between the orders of nature allows scien-

tists to explore the anomalies of classically defined phenomena (e.g., where a vital entity demonstrates a human characteristic) and allows philosophers to sort out the mind-body problem (i.e., there is no problem). Rosen (2008) explains how the mind/body problem only emerges when rigid lines are used to divide nature:

> Yet if the subject, at bottom, is in fact perfectly indivisible thus transcendent of space, and if its objects are completely divisible thus immanent to space, could there be any genuine *interaction* between subject and object? This is of course but another way of stating the old *mind-body problem* that was never quite put to rest in the classical tradition. If mind and body are ontologically divided, how is it possible for them to interact? (pp. 6-7)

He goes on to describe the solution of this problem for philosophers: "[M]ind and body—or subject, object, and space—are not taken as pre-existent, fixed, and mutually exclusive categories. Rather, they are seen to develop in intimate relationship to one another" (p. 7).

## BLURRING THE LINES BETWEEN PHYSICAL, PHYSIOLOGICAL, AND PSYCHOLOGICAL: HUMAN, ANIMAL, AND MACHINE PHENOMENOLOGY WITH GLEN A. MAZIS

Considered above has been Merleau-Ponty's (1942/1963) distinction between the physical, vital, and human orders of nature. These divisions have originally represented a mutually exclusive hierarchy of orders that represent complexity and individual integration in nature. Furthermore, there is some precedent for such division in nature. However, upon closer inspection, the rigid boundaries that have been used to divide nature have proved less clear than anticipated. This is evident even in the arguments of Merleau-Ponty as he seems to have done more to demonstrate similarities across these orders than differences. Finally, this has included an argument for the completion of the shift from classical to contemporary thinking about nature (supplied by Leclerc, 1977). For example, instead of behaving like the inert physical matter the way nineteenth century classic physics would have, physical objects are found exhibiting a dynamic character that makes more sense to be referred to as a process like becoming than the static "is" of mundane inactivity.

Preserved in the above discussion has been the notion that some entities demonstrate higher levels of life, sophistication, individual integration, etc. That is, the dividing lines between orders have come down (or have proven untenable) while maintaining the possibility of degrees of complexity. I am not at once both human and physical entity, but I have the capacity for each. For example, while some entities may exhibit individual integration over longer periods of time, individual integration is a characteristic possessed by all entities in nature. Moreover, that the entity's individual integration is found changing when its milieu changes poses no problems because entities are free to exhibit a variety of levels of individual integration. In this part, a case is made for the absolute collapse of the stratification of nature into degrees of life, sophistication, individual integration, and so on. This is to say that not only are entities made of the same matter, but that physical, vital, and human entities do not necessarily differ in any dramatic way. This is the argument made by phenomenological philosopher Glen Mazis (2008) in a work that has been appropriately titled: *Humans, Animals, and Machines: Blurring Boundaries.* It should be noted that his analysis has been chiefly informed by Merleau-Ponty's phenomenology of embodiment. In the context of the present discussion, it may be understood that Machines represent the classically defined physical order. Mazis writes how "[i]t is a mistake to define humans, animals, and machines as three separate kinds of entities, for there are mechanistic dimensions of animals and humans, as well as animal dimensions of humans and, in some ways, even of machines" (p. 21). Described as such, the orders of nature begin to say nothing about individual entities. An entity does not belong to any given order. Instead, the orders define sets of possibilities for each entity. Insofar as a human's behavior is shaped by rewards and punishments, the entity is a well-oiled behaviorist machine. This, however, does not limit said human to the repertoire of operantly reinforced behaviors.

Mazis explains that such a position has become typical of his life's work. "[P]art of my own writing has been to document the ways in which animality is constitutive of what we think of as most human about ourselves" and the corollary, "how animals express themselves through behaviors and interaction that suggest they have intelligence, feelings, morality, capacities for relationship, and recognition of mortality in certain cases" (p. 5). Since his corpus of scholarship is already available, a complete summary will not be undertaken here. Instead, a brief description will be provided for how he finds the boundaries between life orders to collapse. This includes the collapse of the human/vital boundary as well as the vital/physical boundary. Cobb and Griffin (1977) will be used to further defend this position. It is only through fusing together the orders of nature that any of them may be understood. Not only does this help dissolve the many-millennium-old mind/body problem, but Mazis (2008) argues that it is essential in understanding any and all entities that present in nature. He writes:

> The boundaries of the human, animal, and machine overlap, dance within each other, and separate, or maybe they should separate at certain key moments, but these lines or arabesques have been barely drawn or even traced out for the intricacy and beauty of their movements. Cyborg being—our sense of incorpo-

rating tools, and becoming interwoven with machines within us, about us, and within the meshes of how we have organized the world—has always existed—it is just becoming more literal and extravagant. The animal within us as source of vitality, of joy at organic being, of intercommunion with the creatures around us to experience the planet, is also an ancient aspect of human existence.... (p. 6)

Mazis reminds us that the integral element in understanding nature is interconnection. Beings do not exist in isolation. This is something that Romanyshyn (1982) catches in a lovely quote by Ortega y Gasset (1961): "How unimportant a thing would be if it were only what it is in isolation" (p. 58). Despite several admissions that no such object-in-isolation exists, lines of separation are still drawn. Mazis explains how there is a seemingly arbitrary tendency to demarcate between orders of nature. He attended a conference at Stanford University in 1987 titled "The boundaries of humanity: Humans, animals, and machines." As researchers read their papers, it became clear to him then there was no agreed-upon method for drawing the lines between these orders of nature, or any clear way of differentiating between them!

## Collapsing the Boundary between Physical and Vital Orders

Mazis (2008) recognizes that the key to understanding the collapse of the boundary between physical and physiological orders begins with leaving behind the 19$^{th}$ century notion of matter—the notion that has already been discussed at length above. He provides the following summary of this shift:

> We think of matter as inert, as dumb, as senseless, and as self-contained. Yet what a strange predicament for a material being to fall into—to become closed off to the ongoing communication with other material beings!
> ...Matter is an activity, too, as we are—as animals are, even as machines are. Like us, or these other beings, matter as activity can only be fully understood through tracing its contours and rhythms. Again, we seek to articulate things through time, as we actually live and experience, as the world actually exists, dynamically and evolving in myriad ways. (p. 17)

This should sound familiar by now. The last point he makes, however, has not yet been proposed. It is that physical matter—which is a dynamic activity like water-spiders-gliding-across-a-pond—might be investigated by tracing its contours and rhythms. Note what Mazis has found as the consequence of rejecting the nineteenth century conception of physical matter: even though it is agreed that matter is no longer lifeless and inert, it still isn't taken as a dynamic activity. Though the nineteenth century object has been rejected, there is still carry-over into contemporary conceptions. While they have graduated to active, objects are still considered to be distinct from one another, from their context, and from their milieu. Mazis's bold proposal may be seen explored throughout the remainder of the present work, particularly in chapter five where the posthuman subject must be understood through a variety of transformations wrought by new social technologies.

What remains in collapsing the boundary between physical and physiological orders is the compelling account from Schrödinger (1944/1967) that the organization of the latter far-exceeds the former. Thorpe (1977) summarizes how Schrödinger's account of the unique sophistication of life might also be extended to a thunderstorm. Thorpe does so by quoting Pantin (1968).

> Pantin... points out that almost everything that Schrödinger has said about life could at least in some measure be said about a thunderstorm. A thunderstorm goes on doing something, moving, exchanging material with the environment, and so forth; and that for a much longer period than we would expect of an inanimate system of comparable size and complexity. It is by avoiding the rapid decay into an inert system of equilibrium that a thunderstorm appears so extraordinary. But the parallels between living organisms and thunderstorms, and indeed some other meteorological phenomena, are remarkable. ... Like living organisms, they require matter and energy for their maintenance. This is supplied by the situation of a cold air-stream overlying warm, moist air. This situation is unstable and at a number of places vertical up-currents occur. ... [M]oreover, the storm itself has a well-defined anatomy of what can almost be called functional parts. (p. 2)

The thunderstorm—as well as some other meteorological phenomena—provides a strong example of collapsing the distinction between living and nonliving entities based on characteristics of order, activity, anatomy, and function. To be fair, however, the ellipses in the above excerpt represent the two observed instances of difference between these two orders: spontaneous generation, which the living being cannot do; and evolution, which the nonliving being cannot do (though this one could be argued against from several positions).

In a contemporary example, consider the machine. The machine is built out of discrete parts in a manner that determines its range of capacities. Indeed, it is that after which the machine-metaphor has been based. But if the mechanical system fails as an absolute explanation, what sense is to be made of machines—certainly *they* operate like machines. Mazis (2008) doesn't think so. Even machines resist the classification as mere objects. He writes:

> We could cite the host of machines that now function as tied into "feedback loops" with their environment, a relationship in which events in one play back into the other in a mutual manner, from the simplest thermostat-driven heater or central air-conditioning unit to the most sophisticated medical prosthesis or even to the most prosaic newly marketed vacuum cleaner that moves around the room redirecting itself until it has covered all of its space. (p. 49)

Once again, these examples demonstrate powerful similarities between physical entities and physiological entities. In this description, however, Mazis has used a number of anthropocentric examples. It will be the argument in the later stages of this project that the orders of nature—including machines—may be understood in a way that is not anthropocentric.

In proposing a collapse between the physical and vital orders of nature, Mazis challenges his readers to earnestly consider the consequences that befall an object wrested from the nineteenth century. If it may be recognized that said object is active and dynamic, then certainly it may be recognized that said object participates in activities like other life entities. Thorpe (1977) supplied a summary of the similarities between a thunderstorm and an organism in a way that challenges Schrödinger's separation of living and nonliving beings. And finally, machines were introduced as a new boundary space that challenges the division of nature. Though some work will need to be done here yet. In his comparison between machines and humans below, Mazis (2008) introduces an important step in Artificial Intelligence that has closed this difference a great deal.

## Collapsing the Boundary between the Vital and Human Orders

In collapsing the distinction between vital and human orders, Mazis begins by indicating their similarity on the genetic level. He summarizes Jared Diamond's (1992) findings that humans share a great majority of genetic information. "In this perspective," Mazis writes, "not only are humans not distinct from animals and other chimpanzes, humans 'don't constitute a distinct family, nor even a distinct genus'" (quoting Diamond, p. 4). While this is a surprising bit of information, it is unlikely to make a large impact in contemporary science. Indeed, the appeal is to the nineteenth century mechanical distinction between life-forms. The genetic code guides the physical construction of the organism; if the organism is only the written code, then this is a reduction of the life-form to a mechanism. Suddenly Schrödinger's (1944/ 1967) earlier emphasis on the single- or double-strand of DNA seems misplaced. Again, while the infinitesimal genetic difference between humans and chimpanzees would certainly have astonished nineteenth century communities, it is unlikely to have the division between humans and animals to come crashing down. Here one must look to the capacity of conscious engagement with the world—as in Goldberg's (2009) cortical zone of proximal executive development.

To say that two persons share the same genetic code—much less 98.5 percent of the same code—does not mean that they are the same. Several decades of twin-studies have demonstrated a potential for variability even between identical genetic codes. The differences may be attributed to experiences, contexts, milieu, etc.—because an entity is not determined only by its genetic code but is also shaped by the world. An entity is not independent from its environmental surround. Furthermore, it is not consciousness that allows a body to be shaped by its surround but the reverse.

By focusing on Merleau-Ponty's recognition of the role of the body—not as a classical nineteenth century "mechanism" but a contemporary twentieth century dynamic "becoming"—Mazis observes the range of being that might be occupied by a particular entity. The body actually makes it possible for the orders to overlap entirely. In order to free objects from their nineteenth century limits of finitude and constancy, they must be taken up in this dynamic capacity. When one does so, the segregation of certain objects or bodies into mutually exclusive life-orders falls apart.

> To find the places where humans can be surprised and taken aback by new senses of animals and machines, and of humans in their overlap with animals and machines, as well as to see the suffering of the collisions of these realms, requires entering the depth of the meaning of the material realm "taken in" by the body that binds these beings. (p. 14)

And he continues,

> This means that as embodied beings we are enmeshed in the world with which we relate in such a ways that we are woven into its fabric. If the power of abstract reflection is to *pull away* from being "caught up" in things, to think through the relations of which we are a part from a needed distance, then the body, through perception and the other powers mixed within it, is our *way into* the world (p. 15)

Mazis concludes this line of thought by providing a way out of the nineteenth century mire of abstract object relations. Instead of beginning with the idea that objects are marked by distance and separateness from one another, he suggests that one begins with the capacity of becoming "caught up" in the world. Without a *de facto* separation between psychological capacities of being "caught up" and those of physiological or physical, then the kind of enmeshment with the world with which phenomenologists have grown so familiar may be used to understand the being of other life entities.

It is in recognizing the similarities across life-entities that dissolves the boundaries of their segregation. Entities have bodies. With bodies, entities participate in the world. For each entity, this is an enmeshment *with* the world such that world and entity share in a dynamic event of becoming. Merleau-Ponty (1964/1968) has referred to this as *flesh*. That is, I am a being of nature that can participate in nature because nature and I comprise the same *flesh*. It is in this capacity that Merleau-Ponty may be used to defend the posthumanities. In order to free objects from the nineteenth century prison of isolation and changelessness, they must be allowed to participate as flesh of the world as well. When this happens, the divisions that separate life-entities begin to dissolve. Instead of imposing discrete sets of capacities on discrete entities, these orders instead describe potentialities of particular configurations and assemblages of entities. These capacities are not in principle denied any entity, but exist in each to varying degrees.

## NOTE

## Chapter Three

# The Importance of Resolving
# This Division in Humanistic
# Eco-psychology

When seated at my desk in my office, I am in a world surrounded by my belongings—my things (Applebaum, 1993). Phenomenologists explain how my surroundings are defined by their relationship to me. If a particular object is of no consequence to me, it either disappears into the background, vanishing from my lifeworld or it is even discarded or donated to be taken up by another person. I am the center of and in command of my environment. But when I step outside, I am entering a new world. One that is at once fascinating and frightening. A world that displaces me as the one in control. I am *in* nature. That is to say, I am at home when safe within my home—a space that is secure from the predators, insects, and other surprises of nature. While in nature, I am subjected to its whim and caprice: deer ticks, horse flies, sunburn, and poison oak. These foreign elements of nature impinge on experiences of comfort so I shield myself with repellent and sunscreen, and I kill the poisonous vines in the areas that I choose to frequent. I begin exerting control over bits and pieces of nature. This allows me to be *in* nature for longer and longer periods, which is great because there is something about it that compels me.

The problem that I wish to demonstrate with this hypothetical example is that I am still separate from nature. No matter how deep I travel into the forest, I understand that I am *in* nature. I am the sole subject amidst a host of nature-objects. As objects, I decide their significance to me. Moreover, like the things in my office I get to choose what stays and what goes. This problem is exacerbated further by the assumption that, as a human, I rank higher than these objects in nature. As a result, nature is justifiably exploited by humans for its resources and beauty. American ecopsychologist Will W. Adams (2005) explains how "[w]e live in a culture ideologically and practically obsessed with dominating, controlling, and often annihilating the other-than-human natural world" (p. 113). But the consequences of this anthropocentric exploitation do not begin and end with the nature *out there*. Humans are also affected. And the effects run deeper than anthropocentric concerns—like how squandering fresh water sources will lead to water shortages for future generations of humans. The consequences are experienced now, and it begins with the alienation from nature that has become customary among humans—an alienation that starts with the separation of humans from the rest of nature.

Canadian psychotherapist Andy Fisher (2013) argues that the most important clinical work that needs to be done right now concerns this human-nature division. He writes,

> I have nonetheless wondered at the absurdity of lining up the wounded at the psychotherapists office, and of researching the minutiae of the therapeutic process, while the everyday social forces that violate our nature, and guarantee a steady supply of crippled souls, go for the most part unquestioned—and while these same general forces continue to go about their business of tearing down the biosphere. (p. xiv)

Fisher finds that the fundamental disconnect that is occurring between the aims of clinical psychology and the amelioration of twenty-first century psychological woes stems from the present day ecological crisis. "My conviction […] is that our attempts to come to grips with the ecological crisis will only benefit if we incorporate into them a good, embodied understanding of what kind of creature we are, what our own nature is like" (xv). That is to say, it requires that we recognize that humans are a part of nature: that there is nothing separating humans from nature. If this were recognized, then it would be obvious that we "cannot be studied or cured apart from the planet" (Hillman, 1995, p. xxii); that wilderness is itself restorative to humans (Harper, 1995); or even that the "separation within the human community is deeply reflected in the separation between people and nature" (Anthony, 1995, p. 270). Ecopsychologists have been busily demonstrating the importance of this shift in thinking, but there is still much work to do.

## PREHENSION, NOT APPREHENSION: DE-ANTHROPOCENTRIZING PERCEPTION IN PSYCHOLOGY

When it is maintained that humans are *in* nature, this implies that humans remain separate from nature. To say that humans are *of* nature is to imply that the two are intimately related—indeed, they are defined by this reciprocal interrelationship. Such a move de-anthropocentrizes nature. With it is understood that the significance of nature does not begin and end with its significance to the human. This can be difficult to consider because it asks us to look from a nonhuman perspective. Such a perspective seems to run counter to the mid-century continental philosophies of phenomenology and semiotics—philosophies that attempt to examine nature *through* the nexus of consciousness and language. In these approaches, it is understood that subjectivity is ontologically primary. The essence of nature can only be found through the experiencing subject. When these continental perspectives are paired with anthropocentrism, it is easy to conclude that the significance of nature can only come by way of the human perspective. This is the very problem that French phenomenologist Maurice Merleau-Ponty was struggling against in his notes that were left unfinished (posthumously published as *Visible and the Invisible*). Here he tried to find a way around starting with consciousness. In order to accomplish this, subjectivity must not belong exclusively to the domain of human, but must extend to nonhuman entities as well. Merleau-Ponty accomplishes this in the nonanthropocentric substance he calls *flesh*. Of concern at present is not the human-nature substance, but the interaction of human-nature. As such, I wish to more carefully examine the act of perception in a way that does not privilege the human. English philosopher Alfred North Whitehead will be useful for this task.[1]

Whitehead is a figure that has been popular within the posthumanities movement mentioned above. This is due to his nonanthropocentric process cosmology that centers on his *Concept of Nature* (1925). While many of his peculiar terms would be useful in helping us understand the problematic division between humans and nature, I presently wish to focus on one: prehension (Whitehead, 1929/1978, 1933/1967). Whitehead uses this term to describe the subject-object/human-nature relationship. In the traditional psychophysical definition of perception, a human receives and interprets stimulation from the environment. The object stands by passively until perceived by a human. In that conception the human is responsible for the final meaning-making action, whereas the stimulus remains constant and unchanging. For Whitehead, the psychophysical conception of perception is problematic because it divides a single event into an awareness quality and an object that is cause for the awareness. Nature gets divided into meaning and matter. Whitehead fuses these two into one with his term "prehension." Prehension refers to the single event in which any two entities interact.

Prehension will be useful in understanding the relationships between human and nature in three ways: (1) it provides a single term to indicate the subject-object relationship without demanding that either side of the duality remain stuck in a category; (2) it avoids anthropocentrism as it is a term that applies equally well to humans as well as other subjectivities; and (3) it avoids the assumption that the subject-object action is akin to the problematic "knower-known" that privileges the subject's vantage point—problems that become apparent with subjective action words such as apprehension, knowledge (of), and consciousness (of)—words that suggest the taking of possession.

To Whitehead, the act of prehension recognizes the dynamic interplay of between two occasions who exchange the identities of subject and object. "The subject and object are relative terms" Whitehead (1933/1967, p. 176) explains. "An occasion is a subject in respect to its special activity concerning an object; and anything is an object in respect to its provocation of some special activity within a subject. Such a mode of activity is termed a 'prehension'" (p. 176).

Prehension is not a unidirectional act of meaning making or a psychophysical stimulus-response interaction, it is a mutual interaction. Any entity can be a subject just as any can be an object. Subjectivity is an instance of change brought about by another entity; objectivity is the entity to which the change may be traced. At every moment these two poles have the potential to reverse. In prehension, I do not stand over and above an object giving it meaning, but participate in a dynamic interplay. With prehension, no hard line of separation can be drawn between subject and object because doing so would limit any reciprocity.

## Prehension in the Ecosphere: Hummingbirds at Esalen

By using prehension to describe an experience, an interplay between subject and object is recognized. In it two entities share an experience. The act of prehension does not belong to either. At one moment, an entity provokes an experience in another; in the next, this exchange is reversed. For ecopsychology, this involves the recognition that an individual does not go *into* nature any more than they are inescapably and unagentively drawn forth.

Adams (2015) describes an experience he has during a walk along the grounds of the Esalen Institute that demonstrates the interactive quality of prehension.

> ...I noticed a hummingbird feasting on the nectar of small pink blossoms. Smiling at the dance between the bird and plant, I soon sensed a lively erotic charge throughout the surrounding space—between the hummer and the flowers, and reverberating outward to touch me and be touched by me, as the tiny bird clearly felt me there. The reciprocity grew more intense, and a dynamic intimacy began taking form in two 'places' simultaneously, inseparably: a current of energy/awareness through my whole body.... Then an astonishing event transpired.... I realized the leaves and flower petals were moving in response to the hovering hummingbird. I could actually see the viscous air being pushed down from rapidly beating wings to the green leaves, the leaves bending pliantly in response and then springing back up.... (p. 33)

The hummingbird does not cause Adams's awareness; the flower does not cause the hummingbird's visit; the hummingbird does not cause the vibration of the green leaves. This description cannot be divided into discrete entities sharing unidirectional causal relationships without missing a great deal of meaning. Adams is witness to, then participant in, then forever transformed by the "hummingbird-with flowers-with [him]" event (p. 33). At each defining moment, the entities involved are mutually related—they are co-constituted. The leaves have the capacity of vibration that allows for a certain frequency of hummingbird wing oscillation, which is only found through a reciprocally informing, back-and-forth relationship. Had the leaf been denser, or wet, or even a different color (and thus a different chemical composition with different properties), the resulting back-and-forth relationship would have emerged differently.

Adams uses this example to make a point that is central to problem of the human-nature division: We cannot help but be transformed by our environmental surrounding because it is a part of who we are. Like the hummingbird and leaf, we are participants with nature. Awareness of and attunement to nature has a restorative effect. This restorative effect is in turn directed back toward the community of living things and benefits are shared by all in what Adams calls a "mutually healing (inter)responsiveness" (p. 33). But instead of mutually healing relationships, we find division: "animate nature is being vanquished voraciously and our deep bodily wisdom is ignored" (p. 33).

## Prehension and Apprehension in the Human-nature Relationship

Now that prehension has been defined and described through a few examples, consider the anthropocentric style of perception it replaces—that is, perception as *ap*prehension. With humankind's pathological insistence on controlling and dominating nature, the term "apprehension" is certainly the more familiar of the two. In apprehending an object, a subject seizes and takes ownership of it. Here the subject stands over and above her object. Furthermore, it is understood that the object only has meaning insofar as it has been apprehended and understood by the subject. The meaning of the tree is found in the shade it casts or the timber it provides.

The difference between prehension and apprehension may be compared to the perception of nature as viewed from the "East and West" (Fromm, Suzuki and DeMartino, 1960). As indicated by the title, Zen Buddhist D. T. Suzuki compares the manner by which Nature has been conceived by Eastern and Western thought. He does this by the juxtaposition of two poems. The first is a Haiku written by the Japanese poet Basho (1644-1694), and the second is a short poem written by the English poet Alfred Tennyson (1809-1892). Both poems consider the relationship between subject (human) and object (nature) through the observation of a flower. Basho writes,

When I look carefully
I see the nazuna blooming
by the hedge!

Yoku mireba
Nazuna hana saku
Kakine kana
(Japanese provided for those readers who want to check the poet's parsing of
syllables; p. 1)

For which Suzuki provides the following commentary:

Most Westerners are apt to alienate themselves from nature. They think man
and nature have nothing in common except in some desirable aspects, and that
nature exists only to be utilized by man.

But to Eastern people nature is very close. This feeling for nature was
stirred when Basho discovered an inconspicuous, almost negligible plant
blooming by the old dilapidated hedge along the remote country road, so
innocently, so unpretentiously, not at all desiring to be noticed by anybody.
Yet when one looks at it, how tender, how full of divine glory or splendor
more glorious than Solomon's Kingly attire it is. Its very humbleness, its
unostentatious beauty, evokes one's sincere admiration. The poet can read in
every petal the deepest mystery of life or being. (p. 2)

The expression of the relationship of human and nature found in Eastern
culture is then compared with this relationship in Western culture. Tennyson
is chosen because his poem shares much in common with that of Basho, and
not because he makes a particularly easy target.

Flower in the crannied wall,
I pluck you out of the crannies:-
Hold you here, root and all, in my hand,
Little flower – but if I could understand
What you are, root and all, and all in all,
I should know what God and man is. (p. 3)

Again in commentary, Suzuki explains:

Tennyson... is active and analytical. He first plucks the flower from the place
where it grows. He separates it from the ground where it belongs. Quite differently from the Oriental poet, he does not leave the flower alone. He must tear it
away from the crannied wall, "root and all," which means that the plant must
die. He does not, apparently, care for its destiny; his curiosity must be satis-
fied. (p. 3)

As Suzuki has found them, both poets are interested in the investigation of
nature. Also, both have found the latter just beyond reach. Using the lan-

guage of Whitehead, Basho prehends the nazuna while Tennyson attempts to apprehend the flower in the crannied wall. Apprehension can only occur through the assumption that the poet and the flower are separate, and that a dominant act of capturing must occur. Through his observation, Basho participates in the nazuna event. Tennyson takes up a laboratory relationship with the flower by tearing it from its environmental context and cupping it in his hands.

In the instance of Basho's prehension of the nazuna, space is left for him to be taken under its spell. He is free to become the object that is now drawn forth by the nazuna. The term prehension allows for the reversal of subject and object. Neither entity is locked into a particular ontological identity of subject or object. Basho prehends nazuna; nazuna prehends Basho. Rather than anthropomorphizing the flower, Suzuki anticipates that the shift in activity/passivity as it is experienced by Basho. Basho begins as the explorer—discovering an inconspicuous flower that rests humbly nearby; then a reversal occurs and it is the flower that now demands Basho's admiration. Prehension applies equally to both examples of activity/passivity between Basho and flower.

As told by Suzuki, the similarity between Tennyson's hands-on approach and the modernist conception of Nature is apparent. Just as Whitehead (1938/1958) has observed in the practice of modern scientists, Tennyson has violently torn the flower from its environment in order to investigate it as a discrete, finite object. After the observation has concluded, the flower will be left to die. There is no confusion regarding the roles of knower and known, active and passive, subject and object. Tennyson is the lone subject midst a sea of objects; the former explores while the latter stands passively by.

To be sure, Tennyson enjoys the flower and perhaps gains a personal insight through this exchange, but he has also torn it from the wall. He has exploited nature to his own ends. Furthermore, he does so without compunction! Like the modern human, Tennyson participates in a traumatic natural event, but the significance of this is lost on him because he has dissociated from this identity with nature. However, this does not mean that he does not experience the consequence. It means that he will be forced to ignore or shrug off any subsequent feeling of loss that he might experience rather than acknowledge how the trauma has affected him. This is what Fisher (2013) and Adams (2005, 2015) mean when they describe the dissociation and trauma that result from the division between humans and nature.

## Nature Prehending the Humanities: Abram's Ecological Analysis of Language

American ecologist David Abram (1996) will be used to demonstrate how deep the connection between humans and nature goes—informing what is often assumed to be a quality unique to humans: language!

Abram grew up interested in human perception—particularly the role it plays in shaping reality. He worked as a street magician, transforming reality before the eyes of spectators. His interests in magic as the shaping of perception eventually took him to the worlds of the shamans and healers of indigenous South-Asian villages. These men and women, he reasoned, would be experts in perception because they relied on magic not just to impress others, but to heal them! Here he would certainly learn how to more expertly influence powerful transformations in the perception of reality. However, instead of learning more about shaping the perception of reality, he quickly learned the power of an increased openness to reality. The brilliance of the shamans and healers had less to do with distorting perceptions, and more to do with opening them—imbuing seemingly powerless things with power and life! For example, the duality of living and nonliving was dissolved by expanding the category "living" to include those things that are typically categorized as nonliving.

> Moreover, it is not only those entities acknowledged by Western civilization as "alive," not only the other animals and the plants that speak, as spirits, to the senses of an oral culture, but also the meandering river from which those animals drink, and the torrential monsoon rains, and the stone that fits neatly into the palm of the hand. The mountain, too, has its thoughts. The forest birds whirring and chattering as the sun slips below the horizon are vocal organs of the rain forest itself. (p. 14)

Abram recognizes that Western civilization has imposed an increasingly narrow box around the category of living—a box that effectively separates humans from nature. This has resulted in a decreased awareness of how these other modes of life impact us in personal and meaningful ways—like how witnessing a bulldozer level a small forest can be met with feelings of loss and hurt, or how the extinction of species can occur during our lifetime due to anthropocentric acts of negligence.

Abram explains how we have replaced communication with nature with a system of abstract symbols useful for speaking *about* nature. Where we once spoke *with* nature, we now speak *about* nature. His example of our discourse with and about water demonstrates this nicely. Consider the adjectives that we still use to describe a small creek or stream: bubbling, gurgling, whooshing, and so on. Each of these words sound like the water itself as it bubbles, gurgles, and whooshes. These terms are onomatopoeia: they make the sound they intend to describe. When spoken, these words directly communicate their meaning to an audience. Humans have not imbued nature with language. Indeed, it seems as though the reverse has occurred: nature provides its own language.

Even at the next level of abstraction—the symbolic human representation of these sounds in a lettered format (e.g., "water")—we see a few communicative actions. The "W" in water represents the waves by which water moves. However, at this level of abstraction, it becomes possible to talk about water without referring to any real body of water. Before when someone said "whoosh" they were talking about a particular body of water that communicated something meaningful at a particular time and place. Now it has become possible to say that "water whooshes" and have in mind no actual body of water. This ability to abstract nature into words has shaped our ability to communicate with it. Abram explains how "the more I spoke *about* other animals, the less possible it became to speak *to* them" (p. 25).

## Prehension and the Project of Ecopsychology

The relationship between humans and nature can no longer be understood as a one-way road—that is, as unidirectionally causal. Doing so ignores the reciprocal influence. Humans and nature belong to the same fabric, not different orders that may be arranged in hierarchical fashion. The interrelationship is preserved when human-nature interactions are viewed as prehensions. "The subject matter of ecopsychology is neither the human nor the natural, but the lived experience of interrelationship between the two, whether the 'nature' in question be human or nonhuman" (Fisher, 2013, p. 32).

Anthropocentrism will continue to plague ecopsychology as long as it is maintained that humans are distinct from nature. This will contribute to the pathologies that result from a collective alienation from a nature that is actually quite personal. Whitehead provides language that is effective in helping reverse this trend. His term prehension has been used to demonstrate this. Instead of viewing perception as a meaning-bestowing act where a subject stands over and above her object, prehension recognizes the mutual interrelationship between subject and object. Practicing ecopsychology this way will be difficult because it runs counter to centuries of anthropocentric thinking that has placed humans outside of (and often above) nature. It is time to fuse these back together. "The challenge for ecopsychology is […] to find a mode of discourse that can walk in the challenging space *between* the human and the natural" (Fisher, 2013, p. 32).

Humanistic psychology emerges out of time where it had become customary to reduce human beings to assemblages of mechanisms. They rallied against this trend, finding it dehumanizing—that is to say, the reduction of humanness to part-processes had left something out of the equation. In an effort to justify the reversal of this trend, humanistic psychologists argued that humans belonged to a different category of nature—something that deserved more careful attention than other things in nature. In the middle of this past century, it allowed humanistic psychologists to rescue humankind from the brain-imaging equipment of the biopsychologists and the operant conditioning protocol of the behaviorists, and to discover the complexity of being human. This complexity is no longer in question. Indeed, the phenomenological and ecopsychological examination of this complexity has made it clear that there is more to being human than what is packaged inside the skin. There is a reciprocal interrelationship between human being and the environmental surround. This ontological kinship is ignored if it is maintained that humans are fundamentally distinct from the cities, forests, and mountain ranges in which they can be found dwelling. By maintaining the separation between orders of nature, humanistic psychology has made it impossible to examine an important element of meaning in being a person—specifically the significance of the ecological sphere.

Merleau-Ponty endorses the division of nature into distinct and hierarchically related orders, and provides the reasoning behind doing so. The human order, it seems, needs to remain in a class of its own. However, upon closer inspection the distinct orders that Merleau-Ponty has proposed seem to have more in common than different. His proposed divisions do less to separate nature into distinct orders than to flatten out nature into a single substance! It is understandable that he would later name this substance—that is, flesh.

## NOTE

1. Merleau-Ponty actually arrives at Whitehead's cosmology after publishing *Phenomenology of Perception*, relying heavily upon it in his conception of Nature (2003). The similarity between Merleau-Ponty and Whitehead has been described at length by Hamrick (1999, 2012).

*Chapter Four*

# Problem Two

*Rejecting Non-subjective Forms of Inquiry*

Vignette: In the Spring of 2013, a graduate student presents a paper addressing his mysterious semester-long hiatus from a humanistic psychology department. In what might be compared to the courage required to "come out" sexually in a conservative town in the nineties, this student admits having suffered from debilitating depression, and that (gasp!) he had begun seeking help through pharmacotherapy. The student shared his subjective experience that the biochemical model of psychopharmocology, vilified by humanistic psychologists for the reduction of the human to a system of chemical and biological mechanisms, was integral to his ability to return to the classroom.

The purpose here is not to emphasize what happened next—as if he was then chased away with pitchforks and torches, but in what this setting indicates regarding the culture in which this story was told. The cult of humanism, anxious to situate itself *against* the dictates of mechanized science, strongly suggests that there is an ethical responsibility to the ontological assumptions that one makes regarding health and wellness. While lip-service is paid to methodological pluralism (Baker 1992/2013; Braud and Anderson, 1998; Maslow, 1966), subjective forms of inquiry are venerated while non-subjective styles are vilified. Furthermore, aside from assumptions regarding the etiology of mental wellness, this ethical privilege extends into the appropriateness of content-area, question-asking, and tool-use. For example, as a former instructor in a humanistic psychology department, I routinely had students shamefully express their fascination with biological models of consciousness and their attraction toward statistics-based hypothesis-testing. Students woefully refer to these areas of psychology as 'the other side.' As a cult, the humanistic psychologists deny the benefit of logical empiricist approaches to scientific practice. This in turn limits the sphere of acceptable experiences that humans may have.

Were I to argue *against* this preference for subjective modes of investigation, I would merely be contributing to another generation of oscillating back and forth between mind and body. So instead of arguing in favor once more of the various third-person and objective models of investigation, I argue that we stretch the concept of "subject" so that it includes all possible types of things: not just humans, but tadpoles, cancer, peat moss, and thunderstorms as well. My purpose with this approach is to demonstrate to humanistic psychologists that the same kind of privileges that were bestowed upon humans sixty years ago may be extended to all things. Moreover, I will accomplish this with reference to key figures in the history of humanistic psychology—namely, Maurice Merleau-Ponty and Kurt Goldstein—and concepts in the humanistic psychologist's lexicon like intersubjectivity and self-actualization.

Just like the previous chapter has demonstrated that humans and nature do not belong to different ontological categories, we also find that humans and nature may be understood as exhibiting similar kinds of subjectivity. This doesn't anthropomorphize nonhuman things because it is recognized that this kind of subjectivity precedes humans. Indeed, the argument is that subjectivity, as well as the process of becoming a self, are nonhuman processes.

Nonhumanism has a strong presence in the history of humanistic psychology: it has supplied the concept of self-actualization (Goldstein, 1934/1995). Self-actualization, as neuropsychiatrist Kurt Goldstein has described it, is a central tendency of all life forms. Human beings are no exception. Self-actualization is not unique to humans but may be applied equally to all living things including humans. That is to say, it is a nonhuman attribute in that it applies equally to all things (including humans). This, I have demonstrated (Whitehead, 2017), is perfectly consonant with the work of biosemiotics—an eastern European school of theoretical biology. A look at the work of biosemioticians Jesper Hoffmeyer will conclude this chapter.

Before humanistic psychology can earnestly consider the insights that nonhuman studies might hold, the aforementioned tendency to reject nonhumanistic forms of inquiry must first be addressed.

## THE ANTINEUROPSYCHOLOGY POSITION AND ITS SHORTCOMINGS

There is a tendency in humanistic psychology to reject the insights of related fields such as neuroscience and biology. The above vignette and associated stories captures this. The rejection is not somehow integral to thinking like a humanistic psychologist, but sometimes it is so strong that it is difficult to keep these separated. One such instance of this comes from an article I wrote in 2014 where I provide a pessimistic review of the relationship between neuroscience and psychology. Indeed, it was of the kind of pessimism expressed in Lashley's (1930) lamentations when he wrote that he had "been impressed chiefly by its futility" (p. 1). The shared criticism is that any psychology that relies on insights from neuroscience is in search of a reduction to neuroscience. This is to say that the only available neuropsychology is one that posits that the nervous system causes consciousness, mind-states, emotion, and any other psychological subject-matter. Lashley, Nöe (2009) and myself (2014) have suggested that this neural-correlates model, which operates with a unidirectional arrow of causality, ought to be replaced with a bidirectional arrow of causality. A bidirectional arrow of causality more adequately demonstrates the complex relationship between brain and behavior. It is not enough to say that psychology either relies on neuroscience or that it has nothing to do with neuroscience. The relationship is more complicated than that. A humanistic psychologist needn't choose between being proneuroscience or antineuroscience. The bidirectional arrow of causality—recognizing that cause can go in both directions—avoids the either/or dichotomy. In the pro-/anti-neuroscience debate, it is argued that either mind influences the brain or the brain influences the mind (mind→brain or brain→mind). However, the evidence from neuroscience laboratories suggests that the arrow points in both directions: the body shapes the mind and the mind shapes the body.

Bidirectional causality follows from the immanent ontology of seventeenth century philosopher, Baruch Spinoza (1632-1677). Spinoza (2000; Deleuze, 1970/1988) has been found to be a helpful guide for those reconsidering the traditionally opposing models of science, particularly the area of consciousness theory (Ravven, 2003a, 2003b). Considered thus, neurological and humanistic models of consciousness are both understood to contribute useful and important insights to the understanding of consciousness. However, neither one can claim to have sole dominion over the phenomenon of consciousness.

## Spinoza's Bidirectional Arrow of Causality

In order to understand an alternative consideration of the relationship between psychology and neuroscience, we must first discern the traditional conceptions of causality—"efficient causality" *qua* Aristotle—from the causality as conceived by Spinoza. Deleuze (1970/1988) explains:

> Traditionally, the notion of cause of itself was employed with many precautions, by analogy with efficient causality[...].
> [...] Spinoza overturns tradition doubly since efficient cause is no longer the first meaning of a cause, and since cause of itself is no longer said with a

meaning different from efficient cause, but efficient cause is said with the same meaning as cause of itself. (pp. 53-54)

When Deleuze mentions its "traditional" use, he is referring to causation as it was employed by Galilean and Newtonian physics. Here an effect is determined by its cause. In modern physics, the Aristotelian logical proof holds for physical bodies. For example, if $A$ is the cause of $B$, then the statement 'if $A$ then $B$' would be valid and the statement 'if $B$ then $A$' would not (for one could imagine an instance where $B$ could occur for a reason other than $A$). Efficient causality, in the vernacular of deductive-logically-derived physics, is unidirectional and linear. It is not so with the *Ethics*.

The material iteration of an effect's efficient cause does not exhaust the understanding of what is occurring. Spinoza begins the *Ethics* with the definition, "[b]y cause of itself I understand that whose essence involves existence, or, that whose nature cannot be conceived except as existing" (E1, D1). Now one begins to see the two-part "efficient" causality that Deleuze (1970/1988) has found in Spinoza. On the one hand, the effect on a material body may be traced to its material cause. However, when understanding is limited to these material relations, then one must look back further and further in order to find the first cause. In doing so, one will find that even Newton's laws of motion—the first laws of this causal-relations game as it has played out in modern physics—have taken motion for granted (Heidegger, 1977). On the other hand, one must keep in mind that at the root of an effect is the naturing of Nature—Nature is the cause of itself. A shrewd logician, trained in Aristotelian efficient causation, might identify this as a tautology. Parkinson (2000) explains otherwise,

> [F]or a thing to bring about its own existence, it must first of all exist, i.e., it would have to exist before it exists. Spinoza would reply that this objection presupposes that a cause must precede its effect in time; but this, he would say, is not so. Rather, a cause has to be viewed as a reason—hence is famous phrase 'cause or reason.' (E1 P11; p. 28)

By lumping "cause" together with "reason," one sees that Aristotelian efficient causality is *one* of a possible many (nay, infinite) reasons to explain an effect. This is to maintain that tracing out the material relations between objects—e.g., neurons—would prove insightful. The history of modern science, as Parkinson (2000) observes, has done precisely this:

> The argument is that, over a period of many years, the sciences have made great progress in the discovery of the causes of human actions, and there is no reason to suppose that such progress must stop short of the ability to give a complete explanation of everything that any human being does. (p. 30)

Parkinson maintains the utility of such a project, though this is a limitation of 'causation' as employed by Spinoza. To be sure, Spinoza would not arrest such an enquiry; but he also would not stop with the mapping of material relations of efficient causality. Thus, for Spinoza, one must add the second layer of efficient causality: God. "More exactly, God is the 'efficient cause' of absolutely all things. Spinoza does not define an 'efficient cause'...; he seems to mean by it something that produces or generates its effect" (Parkinson, p. 28, footnote).

Returning to the somewhat cryptic definition that Spinoza has given to cause: an effect, a moment, or an event is always determined by its own essence (*conatus*); and the reverse. Nature natures; how might it be expected to do otherwise? In summary, Deleuze offers a definition and concept that will be used to discuss the dual-mode efficient causality of Spinoza:

> Understood in its one sense and its single modality, the cause is essentially immanent; that is, it remains in itself in order to produce (as against the transitive cause), just as the effect remains in itself (as against the emanative cause). (p. 54)

## LASHLEY'S CRITIQUE OF NEURAL ASSOCIATIONISM

Karl Lashley (1890-1958) was a bold researcher in the areas of biology, zoology, and neuropsychology—publishing some of the first papers on the psychological effects of brain damage. Like Goldstein (1934/1995), Lashley had enough first-personal experience with brain-injured persons to understand that the relationship between cortical matter and experience was not as simple as the modern scientific theories had anticipated. At the time of his (1930) paper, psychology was the newest target for a reductive neurological psychology. Here is Lashley's charming, if tongue-in-cheek analysis of the state of psychology into the mid-century:

> Among the systems and points of view which comprise our efforts to formulate a science of psychology, the proposition upon which there seems to be most nearly a general agreement is that the final explanation of behavior or of mental processes is to be sought in the physiological activity of the body and, in particular, in the properties of the nervous system. The tendency to seek all causal relations of behavior in brain processes is characteristic of the recent development of psychology in America. Most of our text-books begin with an exposition of the structure of the brain and imply that this lays a foundation for the later understanding of behavior. It is rare that a discussion of any psychology problem avoids some reference to the neural substratum, and the development of elaborate neurological theories to 'explain' the phenomena in every field of psychology is becoming increasingly fashionable. (p. 1)

If one has struggled to glean Lashley's opinion of the popular presses, he candidly admits, "I have been impressed chiefly by its futility. The chapter on the nervous system seems to provide an excuse for pictures in an otherwise dry and monotonous text. That is has any other function is not clear..." (p. 1). To be sure, the popularity of sexy full-colored shots of cross-sections of the brain indicating blood-flow patterns has increased even through the twenty-first century (Satel and Lilienfeld, 2013), but Lashley has reduced the importance of neural consideration to this superficial level by arguing that the consideration of the relationship between neurology and psychology is "futile!"

There is some precedent for his concern. As mentioned previously, Lashley was one of the early scholars of associationism. In his studies, he shares his review of many cases of damage to the motor cortex. Lashley explains how associationism works through the analogy of the reflex:

> The starting point for our attempts to account for behavior in terms of nervous processes has been either the cerebral localization of functions or the theory that all nervous integration is patterned after the spinal reflex. I need scarcely point out the difficulties encountered by the older doctrine of cerebral localization. It expresses the fact that destruction of definite areas results in definite symptoms and the probably inference that these different parts have diverse functions, but it has given us no insight into the manner in which the areas or centers exercise their functions or the way in which they influence on another. (p. 2)

If associationism is correct, then irreparable damage to a discrete area of the motor cortex would result in the loss of a discrete motor capability. This, as demonstrated with stroke-patients, is not always the case. Lashley first explains that the nervous system is far more complicated than this theory provides:

> The model for the theory is a telephone system. Just as two instruments can be connected only by certain wires, so the sense organs and muscles concerned in any act are connected by nerve fibers specialized for that act.
>
> Perhaps few neurologists would agree to such a bare statement. They point to the incalculable number of nerve cells, the interplay of inhibition and facilitation, and suggest that in so complex a system there are limitless possibilities. But the fact remains that the essential feature of the reflex theory is the assumption that individual neurons are specialized for particular functions. The explanatory value of the theory rests upon this point alone.... (p. 3)

Next, Lashley explains that the nervous system does not always behave in ways that are conducive to the reflex-theory. Even the firing of a neuron seems to follow rules other than "adequate stimulation." "The adequate stimulus in such cases may be described in terms of a pattern having definite proportions but always, within wide limits, it is a matter of indifference to what receptor cells this pattern is applied" (p. 4). Taken together, the complexity of the cerebral cortex and the limited predictability of the nerves themselves are used as proof that the business of neuro-psychology, save sexy full-page images in textbooks, is futile.

Given the traditional scientific understanding of "efficient cause," Lashley has done well to conclude the project of associationistic neuro-psychology. However, by adding Spinoza's second layer—which Deleuze (1970/ 1988) has termed "immanence"—Lashley's (1930) critique does not extend as far as he might have wished. To be sure, the reflex theory is one *reason* among a possible many that could explain the relationship between bodies (e.g., localized cortical activation→discrete motor action, etc.). Here the [→] stands for the traditional unidirectional cause. Lashley has demonstrated the futility of this approach. What he has missed out on, however, is two-fold. First, by limiting the direction of the causal relationship he misunderstands the nature of a given discrete motor action. Second, by emphasizing associationism by way of the reflex theory, he misses out on the importance of the myriad other material possibilities that exist within the nervous system.

Lashley has considered the accuracy of associationistic neuro-psychology by testing its ability to predict efficient causality. As mentioned above, this has traditionally been that of the variety provided by Aristotle who explains that a cause happens before the effect. If cause, *then* effect. According to the association theory, said motor function can occur *if-and-only-if* (*iff*) the corresponding region is activated. Lashley has noticed that motor function can occur despite the ablation of the corresponding cortical region.

Notice instead what happens when using Spinoza's definition of efficient causality, as interpreted by Parkinson: "something that produces or generates an effect" (2000, p. 28, footnote). We will consider the example of the thumb (Ramachandran, 2011). If a subject has suffered cortical damage localized to the thumb-motor region, then her thumb would be rendered useless. Lashley (1930; and Ramachandran, 2011) have found that the patient is still capable of feeling and manipulating her thumb. Lashley uses this as evidence that neuro-psychology is futile because brain-region *A* cannot be used to explain the cause of motor-function *A*. Bound to Aristotelian efficient-causality, Lashley begins with the cause and looks no further; its use as an explanation is impossible. Spinoza might advocate that Lashley look to the effect: the feeling, moving thumb. Here one finds the 'reason or cause.' Had he done so, he might have discovered what Ramachandran later finds: the thumbing-effect was not limited to the thumb region, but took place on the subject's corresponding cheek. By consulting an associationist diagram of the motor cortex, one finds the thumb-region adjacent to the facial region. The *effect* provided unexpected information for understanding the role played by the brain.

Lashley also misses out on the importance of the complexity of the nervous system. However, much like Heidegger's eye-glasses, he had been staring at them all along. In the previous excerpt, Lashley includes that neurologists "point to the incalculable number of nerve cells, the interplay of inhibition and facilitation, and suggest that in so complex a system there are limitless possibilities." Yet he manages to use this as a reason why the use of the nervous system in understanding psychology is a futile endeavor. Indeed, even in his examples the hundred-million or so nerve-synapses, along with thumbing, conspire against an inert region of cortical matter to affect a cause. I wonder what this might look like if photographed for the pages of an introductory textbook.

## THE APPEAL OF A MODERNIST PROGRAM FOR NEUROSCIENCE: CRICK'S *ASTONISHING HYPOTHESIS*, AND KOCH'S *CONFESSIONS*

Despite the warnings of the futility of material neural-reductionism that have been issued by Karl Lashley, this line of investigation has proceeded undeterred. Indeed, Satel and Lilienfeld (2013) have observed that contemporary society has begun to reflect the scientific preoccupation with the nervous system. They write,

> The media—and even some neuroscientists, it seems—love to invoke the neural foundations of human behavior to explain everything from the Bernie Madoff financial fiasco to slavish devotion to our iPhones, the sexual indiscretions of politicians, conservatives' dismissal of global warming, and even an obsession with self-tanning. (p. ix)

While pop-neurology, apparently sometimes called "blobology" (p. xiii), can be understood by the misunderstandings that inevitably occur when contemporary science reaches the popular presses, the stream of occupations, advanced degrees, and academic disciplines becomes more difficult to reconcile. Satel et al. note the emergence of such disciplines as "neurolaw, neuroeconomics, neurophilosophy, neuromarketing, and neurofinance…"; "neuroaesthetics, neurohistory, neuroliterature, neuromusicology, neuropolitics, and neurotheology" (p. ix). The nervous system has even been used to describe a humanistic—that is, learner-centered—approach to teaching (Whitehead, 2013). This does not mean that it was merely neuro-social-conformity.

Exclusive focus on the brain has characterized the "decade of the brain" (Koch, 2012)—that is, either the nineties or the mid-nineties to the mid-aughts, depending on whom one asks. In any event, it is quickly becoming the "four-score years of the brain" or "quarter-century" of the brain, etc. The depth of conviction regarding the assumption that the brain is the root of all human being can be found between the Nobel winning geneticists: Francis Crick and Christof Koch; the former for his *"astonishing hypothesis"* (Crick, 1994) and the latter for his continued conviction that consciousness may be understood through material reductionism (Koch, 2012). Self-proclaimed neuro-philosopher Alva Noë, whose convictions will be considered at length below, outlines the (astonishing) hypothesis of Crick. "You, your joys and your sorrows, your memories and your ambitions, your sense of personal identity and free will, are in fact no more than the behavior of a vast assembly of nerve cells and their associated molecules" (Crick, 1994; cited in Noë, 2009). The last line really demonstrates the depth of conviction of a neuro-material reductionist. Humanity is "nothing but" the nervous system. Satel et al (2013) address the main appeal and concern of such an assumption:

> More complex than any structure in the known cosmos, the brain is a masterwork of nature endowed with cognitive powers that far outstrip the capacity of any silicon machine built to emulate it. Containing roughly 80 billion brain cells, or neurons, each of which communicates with thousands of other neurons, the three-pound universe cradled between our ears has more connections that there are stars in the Milky Way. How this enormous neural edifice gives rise to subjective feelings is one of the greatest mysteries of science and philosophy. (p. xi)

The problem that requires reconciliation to the material reductionists is subjective experience. If humans are, indeed, "nothing but" their nervous systems, then how do we make sense of exasperation, benevolence, and musicality; in the parlance of consciousness theory, how does a "quale," the smallest unit of experience, occur? In philosophy of mind, this is referred to as the mind/body problem. How can a material body—which can be understood and explained by thermal physics, molecular biology, and other empirically-based modern natural sciences—be said to influence a thought or an idea—notions that can be understood through intellectualism, rationalism, and various other non-empirical disciplines?

In the context of the present discussion, the avenue of understanding will be in terms of causation or reason—that is, what is the reason or cause that such-and-such is the case. We have introduced two types of causal explanations: Aristotelian *efficient causality*, and Spinozist "reason or cause." As indicated by Deleuze (1970/1988) and demonstrated by Lashley (1930), the traditional mode of explanation is of the Aristotelian *efficient causality* ilk. As such, this is how the mind/body problem is reconciled: One must first decide which substance comes first, mind or body. Having decided this, the onus of explanation will be on the primary substance in the determination of the second substance. For example: if the mind is primary, then bodily effects must be explained with the mind. These might include will, intention, motive, etc. If the body is primary, then these seemingly autonomous intellectual processes—that is, the mind—must be explained as effects of the body. These might include habit, impulse, brain-association, etc.

Crick (1994) and Koch (2012) have astonishingly and confessedly taken up the primacy of the body—specifically the brain. Once again, Crick has indicated that joys, sorrows, memories, ambitions, and free will are nothing more than nerve-cells. By beginning with the body, one may understand everything that there is to know about the list of seemingly intellectual, spiritual, or rational processes. Similarly, Koch shares his anticipated solution to the "quale" problem in consciousness: "I believe that qualia are properties of the natural world. They do not have a divine or supernatural origin. Rather, they are the consequences of unknown laws that I would like to uncover" (p. 28). That is, experience will eventually be understood in terms of the relationships between material bodies—neurons, for example.

Material neuro-reductionism presents two problems given the premises of the present discussion. First is the unidirectional, *if-and-only-if* causal relationship between nerve-tissue and experience. For example, given Lashley's (1930) "limitless possibilities," Crick and Koch are interested in narrowing it down to Occam's single cause. The second problem is the status given to experience, thoughts, feelings, rationality, etc.: they are second-order or epiphenomenal to workings of the brain.

Very little has to be done in order to address these two problems. Indeed, material reductionists need only acknowledge the limited scope entailed by the first problem, and the neglect of thought entailed by the second. Beyond this the material reductionists are free to find as many single causes for as many single experiences as their tools allow. They simply will be unable to say that they have exhausted all possible causes—will be unable to arrive at a universal ontological framework. As Parkinson (2000) mentioned above, the material reductionists need not discontinue their project just because they cannot conclude with a "complete explanation of everything."

The material reductionists will continue to do their thing, the popular presses will continue to misconstrue their findings, and doctoral students will continue to proudly present bold and daring, if myopic papers at regional conferences. Remarkably, meaningful insights will still be gleaned by students, bus drivers, and corporate secretaries from all manner of internet blogs, impromptu coffee-house seminars, and TEDTalks that chronicle the bourgeoning neuro-century. Despite the candor with which Koch (2012) has portrayed his material reductionist commitments, even he will take it personally when his son admits that he prefers the company of video games to that of his father.

REFUTING THE MATERIAL NEURO-REDUCTIONISTS: NOË
TRADES THE ONTOLOGICAL PRIMACY OF THE BODY FOR
THAT OF SUBJECTIVITY

With an anthology of anomalous neurobiological case-studies in one hand, and a celebratory humanitarian flag in the other, Alva Noë (2009) proudly proclaims that *You Are not Your Brain*. Like Lashley, Noë has compiled an impressive number of evocative examples of how the Modernist neuroscientific project fails as a comprehensive system of explanation. In terms of the preceding discussion—namely, Spinoza's "reason or cause"—there is no question that any comprehensive system of explanation is going to fail. For the Modernists, the point is not to identify the sum-total of possible material relationships, but to see what is learned when this project is earnestly undertaken. However, like Lashley before him, Noë does succeed in pointing out how this kind of a task would be infinite. Once again, this is no reason to give up the effort.

Unlike Lashley (1930), Noë (2009) does not simply shake his head and say "huh uh" at the material neuro-reductionists; he proposes an alternative comprehensive system of explanation. Instead of indicating the primacy of the nervous system, Noë defends the primacy of the embodied-subject:

> [T]o understand consciousness in humans and animals, we must look not inward, into the recesses of our insides; rather, we need to look to the ways in which each of us, as a whole animal, carries on the processes of living in and with and in response to the world around us. The subject of experience is not a bit of your body. You are not your brain. The brain, rather, is a part of what you are. (p 7)

Noë explains that the "mind/body" problem is more difficult than simply picking a side. Heavily influenced by Merleau-Ponty (1942/1962), Noë outlines an intentional consciousness that begins with the primacy of perception. Perception co-constitutes a subject and her environment. It is through perception that both subject (mind) and object (body) become. Like Merleau-Ponty before him, Noë comes dangerously close to defending an immanent causality where body and mind, subject and object are understood to be reciprocally effected-affecting. Instead, Noë is left with a sophisticated dualism. The case has also been made that Merleau-Ponty's initial courageous trek into non-duality came up short as well (Barbaras, 1991/2004; Merleau-Ponty, 1964/1968). Look instead at the trip-up committed by Noë: "You are not your brain. The brain, rather, is a part of what you are." What/where is the subject? Backing up a few lines, Noë assumes the unified whole-animal. Are we to imagine that subjectivity is thus relegated to whole animals? Or is it, perhaps, in the reverse? Instead of looking to the brain for a reductive definition of being, consciousness, and humanism, Noë has looked to the subject.

To be sure, the book is a compelling case for what can be learned, understood, and demonstrated about experience through Humanist neuroscientific project. But, like Crick and Koch, Noë has limited the quest of understanding serendipity, infomercials, and bicycle gain-ratios to a single system of explanation: the intentional embodied-subject. Noë, along with the human-subjectivity-bound phenomenologists (Harman, 2011), have erected a universe around the assumption that the latter is either for human-subjectivities or, no less anthropocentric, may only be meaningfully understood through human subjectivity. In this sense, Noë's science of the embodied subject is no less limited in possibilities than is material neuro-reductionism. Once more, this should do nothing to dissuade the phenomenologists from asking their penetrating questions to war veterans, ESL students, and micro-economics professors. Indeed, ask away. While their findings may not make it into the blogs the same ways neurofanaticism has, insights will certainly trickle through to the unsuspecting philosophy undergraduates and the parents of their professors.

The limited humanistic scope only precludes this brand of neuroscience from being a complete system of explanation. Recall that this too was the case with the Modernist neuroscientific project. But one still finds the problem of the unidirectional causal arrow. While embodied subjectivity takes measures to collapse the split between mind and body, Noë still speaks of the brain that is part of the imperious subject. Everything that comprises the subject—which, Noë allows, extends beyond the skin-boundary—exists only in the intentionality of the subject. The brain, tendons, and intestinal villi all participate in the subjectivity of which they are constituents. Even if they could be investigated individually, the independent learnings could not possibly add up to the capital-s-Subject since, following the lead of Köhler (1947/1957) and the Gestaltists, "the whole is greater than the sum of its parts." Thus, my fingernails, eyelids, and shoulder-blades do not participate in my projects until I perceive them as doing so. Until I apperceived it to write this sentence, the family crest hanging on the wall behind my head did not exist; I intended it as part of my expository project, after which it will fade away into oblivion along with the electric wall-sockets, *The Brothers Karamozov*, and toaster-ovens.

This results in a strange conversation between phenomenology and neuroscience—popularly called neuro-phenomenology. Each side, sticking faithfully to its ontological commitments, sees the other with a limited perspective. To the humanists, nerve-cells, DNA, and enamel belong to the subject in her singular being-in-the-world. The degree to which the former subject-constituents matter to the subject is limited to the latter's subjective awareness. Thus, conferring with any of the hundred million-billion neural synapses that comprise the subject (Seung, 2012; counting, I suppose, only those within the subject's skin) would be largely fruitless. Since they comprise the subject and are not subjects themselves, their contributions would be nothing more than the subject could have reported in the first place. To the Modernist, subjective reports are only insightful insofar as they can be reliably mapped by their available tools. For the fMRI, the imaging technique that yields the most discriminating data, this amounts to detectable traces of blood flow and oxygen consumption by regions of the brain. Ontological privilege is given to what is happening in the brain. Subjective reports are then appended to the neural happenings with the skeptical objectivist-scientist bent: subject *reported* feeling, having, experiencing, etc.

## TOWARD A NEUROSCIENCE BASED IN SPINOZA'S NOTIONS OF CAUSALITY

The battle between material neuro-reductionism and anthropocentric-subjective-reductionism is only a battle when it is presumed that the winner will have defended a complete explanatory system. Ravven (2003) explains the circumstance, "We suppose that our desires and reason, *i.e.,* our body and mind, are locked in a battle for control of our will" (p. 70). For Modernism, this is one that begins and ends with the smallest observable material body; for Humanism, one that begins and ends with an intentional embodied-subject. A complete explanatory system only exists when Aristotelian *efficient causality* is the chief method of explanation. As explained in commentary to the above positions, there would be no battle had each of these positions acknowledged their necessary limitations as explanatory systems. That is, had they employed Spinoza's causation—"reason or cause"—then nothing would have to have been sacrificed regarding their own investigations, but they would likely have been able to begin an inter-disciplinary dialogue in a neutral territory of similar experimentation. For example, material neuro-reductionism generates insights; anthropocentric-subjective-reductionism generates insights; what happens when put together?

Ravven suggests that Spinoza provides an alternative to this recurring battle:

> All these standard assumptions upon which we build our ethical life, we are now beginning to realize, may be false. Baruch Spinoza, a somewhat younger contemporary of Descartes, challenged these assumptions back in the seventeenth century and reconceived ethics, contra Descartes, upon what is turning out to be a rather sound biological basis. We have much to learn from him even today. Spinoza's doctrine was a radical but non-reductive psychophysical monism, a mind-body identity theory that reduced neither body to mind nor mind to body. The mind, he said, fundamentally minded the body and he maintained the causal efficacy of both the mental and the physical. (p. 70)

Ravven's description of Spinoza sounds a lot like the combination neuro-phenomenologist without the respective ontological commitments. Phenomenologists might start cheering and toasting after the identity bit where "the mind...minded the body" and ignore the rest, while neuroscientists would be too busy sighing in relief after hearing "Spinoza's...mind-body identity theory that reduced neither body to mind" to hear that the mind wasn't to be reduced to the body either. Instead of requiring that *either* the brain be first *or* the subject be first, what would happen if Spinoza's "reason or cause" were taken up in a radical "non-reductive psychophysical monism." Consider what this might look like. A scientist that is open to, even enamored with, the possibilities demonstrated by the phenomenologist. But then turns around and listens with similarly rapt attention to the neuroscientist. Without a commitment to either/or, a Spinozist scientist could explore both, and even be present to the possible interconnections. Compelled to provide a simile, I will do so without discrimination. For the anthropocentric-subjective-reductionists, this might be like a well-behaved, middle-class American Christian child on Christmas morning; for the material reductionists, this might look like a dancing valence-electron of an alkaline-element.

## EXAMPLES OF NONHUMANISTIC PSYCHOLOGY

### The Nonhuman Self: Jesper Hoffmeyer's Biosemiotics of Becoming a Person

The psychology of the early twentieth century managed to ignore its very subject matter—namely, the person. William James, the first psychology faculty member at an American University, preferred to classify himself as a philosopher so as not to be associated with American psychologists had been doing. As summarized above as "neural associationism," it had become increasingly common to view humans as assemblages of biological mechanisms. Add these assemblages up and you get a person.

Like many biologists and neurologists at the time, humanistic psychologists maintained that there was more to being a person than simply adding up all of the component parts. All of these parts work together and in service to a far more complicated process—the process of becoming a self, or self-actualization. Self-actualization becomes the background context only within which a person's symptoms might be understood. In early twentieth century psychology, the person is what you get after you put all the simple psychological elements together. Humanistic psychologists were learning that you must begin with the person in order to understand the constituent psychological elements.

The fact that self-actualization comes from a solution to a neurological problem is easily lost in how empowering this is to humanistic psychology.

Self-actualization is tendency of all organisms, not just humans (Goldstein 1934/1995; 1963). Biology is responsible for the concept of self-actualization, not humanistic psychology. Indeed, contemporary theoretical biology still has much to offer humanistic psychology. The reverse is also true.

Jesper Hoffmeyer is a theoretical biologist that studies biosemiotics. Like humanistic psychology, biosemiotic study begins with the assumptions that behavior cannot, in principle, be reduced to simpler and still more fundamental elements: context, situation, and organism must each be considered as integral to an organism's behavior. Furthermore, life must be understood as a network of relationships whereupon organisms always participate in meaningful, and meaning-making, behavior. However, these behaviors must be understood intersubjectively. The overlap between biosemiotic theory and self-actualization in humanistic psychology has been carried out more thoroughly elsewhere (Whitehead, 2017).

Biosemioticians are similarly critical of the Aristotelian principle of efficient causality in Netwonian science. Like human beings, molecular structures are not pre-programmed to complete a certain repertoire of behaviors, but may be better understood as "potential sign vehicles mediating communicative activity between cells, tissues, and organs of our body or between bodies" (Hoffmeyer, 2014, p. 95). For Hoffmeyer, "All organisms on Earth are descendants from symbiotic conglomerates of bacterial cells" (p. 101). He has previously explained the bacterial production of self-regulation, personhood, and psychology in humans as well (2008, pp. 213-261).

Biosemiotics examines organic life the same way a human science researcher (for example, a phenomenologist) might example the experience of a human. Both researchers begin with a complicated network of meaningful interrelationships between the subject of study and its environment—this is called the *Umwelt* or "lifeworld." While my toothbrush might be a tool that is useful for protecting against gingivitis and tartar build-up, it is also part of a bedtime ritual that I complete with my wife. The meaning of the ritual is not given in the tool itself, but can only be seen when viewed within the entire context within which the event unfolds. Following German biologist and zoologist Jakob von Uexküll, biosemioticians such as Hoffmeyer have found it best to view all biological activity this way. The biosemiotic model "points us to emphasize relational phenomena that, in principle, are independent of the substantiality of the related entities, and this opens new channels of explanation" (Hoffmeyer, 2014, p. 103).

Hoffmeyer is not arguing for a nonhuman noetic phenomenology (Husserl's examination of subjective experience; 2002). Instead, he argues that the meaningful organization of an *Umvelt* (lifeworld) is a nonhuman tendency. It hasn't started with humans; it has preceded them. A thinking thing, where thinking may be understood as the ability to meaningfully interpret signs and symbols, may be found "in the very basic senso-motoric *unity* of all animal multicellular life" (p. 233). Hoffmeyer continues, "Nothing could be more backwards... than to understand *human* cognition as the primary or most definitional form of cognition" (p. 233).

In sum, biosemiotics represents just one area of nonhuman inquiry. This does not mean shedding the details of meaning, intersubjectivity, lifeworld, or holism. The more carefully that scientists look, the more complicated life seems even at cellular levels. Humanistic psychologists are not alone in their search to understand the meaningful organization of experience. "Living creatures are not just senseless units in the survival game; they also *experience* life (and perhaps even "enjoy" it as we say when human animals are concerned)" (Hoffmeyer, 2008, p. xiii). To be sure, biology stands much to gain from human science methods (such as phenomenology, Rosen, 2015). But the human science methods may also stand to gain something from biology (Whitehead, 2015).

## Neurophenomenology of Francisco Varela

Francisco Varela (1946-2001) was a South American biologist who studied with Humberto Maturana. The two of them wrote *Autopoiesis and Cognition* together. In this text, as described by the edition editors, the authors "propose a theoretical biology... from the 'point of view' of the system itself" (Cohen and Wartofsky, 1972, p. v). That such a view was unprecedented within the field of biology at the time can be seen in the quotation marks placed around "point of view," as though such a perspective is inherently silly. But Maturana and Varela accomplish precisely this.

Varela became a highly respected biologist, but never left behind the philosophical and theoretical problems that plagued biological science. He was active in creating interdisciplinary collaborations where, for example, the ideas of religion, philosophy, biology, and neuroscience could intersect. As an example of this he co-founded the Mind and Life Institute (1987) where leading researchers to this day still convene to discuss relevant intersections between contemporary science and Buddhist religion.

Varela's intuition that something important was missing from the research into consciousness could be found in a chapter he wrote for an edited volume of papers delivered at a conference on "The Science of Consciousness" (Hameroff, Kazniak, and Scott, 1997, pp. 31-44). In it, Varela argues for an increased emphasis on experiential, first-person accounts. That is, consciousness from the 'point of view' of the person. He never abandoned the importance of experience as a fundamental, biological attribute. His proposal for "neurophenomenology" (1996) is an attempt to minimize the alleged gap between first-person and third-person observations. To maintain such a division between first- and third-person accounts ignores how "so-called third-person, objective accounts are done by a community of people who are embodied in their social and natural worlds as much as are first-person accounts" (1997, p. 38).

*Chapter Five*

# Subjectivity as a Nonhuman Attribute

## *All Nature as* Flesh

There still remains a difficult area of reconciliation that emerges as soon as one attempts to fit humanistic psychology within the category of nonhuman studies. It is the relationship between subjectivity and objectivity. It can be summarized as follows: what becomes of the study of subjectivity when it can no longer be kept separate from the studies of objectivity? Merleau-Ponty, who was helpful in collapsing the boundaries between life-forms in the previous chapter, will be used once more. This time his concept of "flesh" will be used.

From the perspective of modern science, objectivity is the actual, third-person verifiable observation of reality. Subjectivity can only be validated from a first-person perspective. It is how something seems from a particular vantage point. In the previous chapter, there were a few examples of biologists who challenged this relationship between subject and object. Hoffmeyer, the biosemioticians described molecular organisms (once relegated to the world of objects to be viewed through microscopes) as being capable of exercising volition and having experience. Varela argued that third-person observations cannot occur except through subjective awareness. This chapter will take these arguments further, arguing that the designations of subjectivity and objectivity do little to differentiate between entities. The customary division between subjectivity and objectivity may be understood much like the customary divisions of nature in chapter 3: they share more similarities in common than they do differences.

## SUBJECTS AND OBJECTS

From a modern science perspective, and object is anything that exists in fact
and is impotent to act. Objects are passive, but they may be acted upon.
Objects are the coffee-cups, dry-erase boards, and fencing swords: they sit
still until they are acted upon. Subjects are those that move about an environment, free to interact with objects. Subjects are active, and may take possession of an object. Subjects are the toddlers, first-base umpires, and high
school vice-principals. On one side there are the passive objects, on the other
the active subjects. Or so it was believed.

Though it has been customary to keep them separated, I argue that subjects and objects may be found folding into one-another and overlapping in
what Merleau-Ponty (1964/1968) has termed *flesh.* The coffee that is slowly
soaking into the fibers of my jeans is not just taking up the space of its
container (as physicists have said of liquids), but interacting with the material
properties of denim with its own chemical and material properties. The event
will occur indefinitely, beginning with a shout of surprise (from me), and
continuing into the no-longer-discernible stain of something that may have
happened once.

The overlapping between (supposedly) independent events occurs to such
a degree that the continued discussion of separation within an event becomes
increasingly impossible. Understood as *flesh,* it may instead by understood
that subjects and objects overlap, and that an observer must admit that she
has trouble deciding on which side of the subject-object duality each part
belongs. Indeed, it soon becomes understandable to flatten these categories
entirely—that is, to speak of the subjectivity of objects and the objectivity of
subjects. Philosopher and cosmologist Alfred North Whitehead (1929/1978;
1933/1967) prefers to use the term "prehension" to describe the mutuality of
the subject-object relation in a way that supplies ontological privilege to
neither. The "active" subjects are no more important than the "passive" objects. This expands the population to whom subjectivity and consciousness
applies.

When the collapse between the supposedly mutually exclusive categories
of "subject" and "object" takes place, we find that subjectivity begins to
leave behind the traditionally human subject and consciousness begins to
leave behind the traditionally conscious human. For example, Merleau-Ponty
(1964/1968) has proposed that consciousness need not be limited to a human
totality, but may be understood as emanating from appendages or even tissue. Moreover, the question of objective or subjective continuity—that is,
how something persists through time—must also be raised. Whitehead, for
example, prefers to describe this process of individuation in a way that applies to humans as well as atoms (1933/1967, p. 177). In expanding the
notions of subjectivity, objectivity, consciousness, and sentience, the subject

of psychological investigation is found necessarily embedded in a particular milieu, existing only as a constituent of the present moment. Suddenly the biologies of Hoffmeyer, Maturana, and Varela begin to seem less and less far-fetched.

## MERLEAU-PONTY'S *FLESH*

French philosopher Renaud Barbaras (1991/2004) finds that Merleau-Ponty, particularly in *Visible and the Invisible*, presents a monist ontology: that humankind and nature are of the same substance. The last chapter has demonstrated how, even in Merleau-Ponty's earlier work, there were more similarities between humans and nature than there were differences.

Barbaras writes how "Insofar as it is a return to the originary field of experience, philosophy must provide itself with a way of speaking that allows to appear both that about which it is speaking and that which is speaking in it" (p. xxix). We cannot continue to have two manuals (or vocabularies) to which we must refer when speaking about reality: the manual that applies to the qualities possessed by objects and the manual the applies to the sense-capabilities of subjects. We need to replace this pair of manuals with a single manual that applies to nature. The reader examines the text so as to decipher its meaning, but then the text draws the eyes here and then, transforming the awareness of the once autonomous reader in a way that very much objectifies the latter. A single manual for understanding such an experience might maintain that the words that have been printed onto this page are just as responsible for your eye-saccades as your intentional consciousness.

By centering on the paradoxes as they arise in the human subject, Merleau-Ponty begins to see the intertwining across sensible and sentient entities. Hands can be the vehicle of sense-perception—the ambassadors of human subjectivity. But at the very next moment they can become objects to be sensed. Merleau-Ponty continues,

> [T]o decide for this reason alone that our hands do not touch, and to relegate them to the world of objects or of instruments, would be, in acquiescence to the bifurcation of subject and object, to forego in advance the understanding of the sensible and to deprive ourselves of its lights. We propose on the contrary to take it literally to begin with. We say therefore that our body is a being of two leaves, from one side a thing among things and otherwise what sees them and touches them; we say, because it is evident, that it unites these two properties within itself, and its double belongingness to the order of the "object" and to the order of the "subject" reveals to us quite unexpected relations between the two orders (p. 137)

Instead of requiring that hands, cornucopias, and bicycle helmets be neatly sorted into categories of sensing and sensed, Merleau-Ponty recognizes that their categorical identities are always on the verge of reversing. Naturally, reversibility makes the placement of subjects and objects, sensing and sensed into neatly defined categories impossible. This is because their classification is contingent on the event in which the entities are found at a particular moment. However, as soon as they are identified in the role as subject or object, the event has already passed. Being a subject means that *in the previous moment* one's relation was one of being aware of and interacting with an object. Being an object means that *in the previous moment* one's relation was one of being the ground upon which a subject was made aware. This leaves the former object-entity to take on a subject-entity role and vice versa.

Merleau-Ponty (1964/1968) has suggested that the term *flesh* stand in for the mutuality of subject-and-object interrelations. It is a word that does not assume a collapse of duality, yet recognizes the fuzzyness with which these categorized entities present themselves. For Merleau-Ponty, flesh is "an element, as the concrete emblem of a general manner of being" (p. 147). *Flesh* is the kernel of ontological possibility.

To understand *flesh,* Merleau-Ponty (1964/1968) has indicated that perception is an insightful place to start. Moreover, insofar as the present project is interested in remaining within the discourse of psychology, the psychophysical event of perception provides an apt starting point. It is in our perceptions that the element of flesh makes itself present. In dialogue with a neighbor or even in a walk through the woods there is reciprocal interactivity. Perception is our attunement with our environment. Perception is the vehicle of engagement with the environment. Walking along a country road our awareness begins to settle onto an ambiguity—at first a formless but curiously unsettling mass, and next a certain and alarming rattlesnake! As we lean in closer to get a better look, the snake reorients her body—leaving the defensive position of motionlessness and taking an offensive position—at this we find ourselves taking up a position of defense, and so on. We are an object of thermal perception to the rattlesnake subjectivity; the rattlesnake is an object of visual awareness to human subjectivity. Our exchange is one of intersubjectivity, or what Tom Sparrow (2015) has deanthropocentrically called "intercorporeity."

Intersubjectivity describes perception as a discourse with nature. With it the boundaries of individuality between subject and object begin to deteriorate. Indeed, the falling acorn takes hold of the subject's awareness as the latter awaits the resolution of the ambiguity of the noise in an otherwise quiet forest. This intertwining is less unusual in the visual and musical arts. In a rare excursion outside the artistic realm of Impressionist painting, Merleau-Ponty (1964/1968) describes the intertwining of violinist and sonata. We are not in possession of the music, he writes, "they possess us" (p. 151). The second-chair violinist is subservient to the sonata that emerges around and through her. So too is the sheet of music. The music-stands, formal attire, and the couple in row E, seats three and four are in harmony—they are each singular participants to, as well as constituent parts of the sonata; they togeth-er comprise the *flesh* of the sonata. If the couple were to suddenly stand up in the middle of the song, we can be sure that the rhythm of the auditorium would be significantly altered. "[T]he moments of the sonata," Merleau-Ponty tells us, "adhere to one another with a cohesion without concept, which is of the same type as the cohesion of the parts of my body, or the cohesion of my body with the world" (p. 152). Just as the body has levels of organization that increase in complexity—cells, tissues, organs, organ-sys-tems, and so on each unified as a single body—so too does the sonata have many elements that may be understood in their own right, but are also mean-ingfully understood within the context of the entire sonata of which they are an important part.

Examples from the arts like this one provided by Merleau-Ponty are common enough to experience, but how about the more mundane activities such as buttoning up one's shirt, loading the dishwasher, or making the necessary arrangements to fly from Atlanta Hartsfield-Jackson International Airport to Gerald R. Ford International Airport: do these activities also lend themselves to such reversibility? Given the ubiquity of these activities, Mer-leau-Ponty has found them to be the best place to start.

Instead of investigating the familiar and easily imagined instances of losing awareness of one's self to meet the demands of a novel, a painting, or a child's first words, Merleau-Ponty gives as an example the most mundane sense-activity imaginable: touching one hand with the other. It is an exercise that anybody reading could immediately put to practice. With it, Merleau-Ponty demonstrates the reversibility of *flesh* through the inter-, intra-corpo-real tactile sense-contact between hands. This is the set up: using your right hand, touch something with which you do not identify as part of your person. Notice the investigative sense-action of hand touching in addition to the investigated sense-object. Here we have two parts to the subject-object unity: right-hand-subject with sense-object (Whitehead, 1929/1978, refers to this as the subject-superject unity). Merleau-Ponty calls this part "right hand touch-ing the things." He argues that the sensorial relationship between right hand and things is only possible because both entities are united in *flesh*. This could certainly mean that the investigated objects are sensing one's right hand, but such an experience can only be substantiated by speculation. True reversibility can only be experienced by the human subject who is simultane-ously aware of her/his capacity for sensation and sentience.[1]

Here is how reversibility may be demonstrated by the human subject: Introduce your left hand to the present experiment and attempt the following: Touch your "right hand touching the things." That is, while maintaining the identity of right-hand-subject, introduce a left-hand-subject. Merleau-Ponty explains what the experimenter no doubt finds:

> My left hand is always on the verge of touching my right hand touching the things, but I never reach coincidence; the coincidence eclipses at the moment of realization, and one of two things always occurs: either my right hand really passes over to the rank of touched, but then its hold on the world is interrupted; or it retains its hold on the world, but then I do not really touch it—my right hand touching, I palpate with my left hand only its outer covering. (p. 148)

After attempting part two of the do-it-yourself reversibility exercise, the role of "right hand touching things" has reversed and it becomes a thing touched itself. Either this reversal occurs or the left hand proves impotent to exercise a sensuous investigation of the right hand and remains at the rank of touched. The sentience of each handed-activity remains distinct from the other; there are two sensing appendages. Their relationship, despite efforts at coordination, remains one of opposition—touching or touched. But their respective roles of touching then touched fold over and across one another with such frequency and clarity that it becomes impossible to assign a singular identity of "touched" or "touching" to either. As *flesh*, the opposition of touching-and-touched recognizes the diversity of nature's interrelationships without discarding the mutuality of the entities involved. That is, it may be understood that there is a distance between sensing and sensed, but as soon as one begins to assign entities to either side of the dualism one runs into a problem: the reversibility of *flesh*, which spans across these ontological chasms, prevents any singular relational identities. This is because a single event does not forever restrict an entity to any particular identity. A subject-entity may subsequently be found playing the role of an object, beckoning another entity as subject into the subject-object relationship. Consider how the protagonist of Pirsig's *Zen and the Art of Motorcycle Maintenance* might endeavor to slice apart experience with his Platonic scalpel, dividing it into piles labeled "subject" and "object." First up is the violinist and sonata. The language with which they are spoken presents a perforated line for their easy separation into violinist:sonata. Now which goes where? Given the reversibility across and between this dualism that has already been discussed, our metaphysician has two options: (1) create a third category of "uncertainty" or (2) place both entities in each of the categories. Platonic forms are irrecusable in present-day Western thought; experience can always be thus divided. However, this does not mean that entities will unambiguously present themselves as one or the other. One finds that entities in nature exhibit the properties and characteristics of both *natura naturans* and *natura naturata*.

## SUBJECTIVITY OF *FLESH* AND SUBJECT-LESS SUBJECTIVITY

Merleau-Ponty has thus far been used to describe several occasions of the dynamic and static interrelations between subjects and objects. When allowing for the reversibility between the roles of subject and object—roles that forever stand opposed to one another as passive and active—attention has been given to the impact had on the human in perception.

Now it is time to take this a step further: can we understand the "experience" of nonhuman individuals? Jesper Hoffmeyer (2008, 2014) and Humberto Maturana et al (1972) think that you can. Perception with and of the human body will be used to extend the notions of subjectivity and consciousness beyond their singular organismic totality. This has been demonstrated in the act of perception in two ways. First, Merleau-Ponty has demonstrated how the roles of subject and object are always on the verge of reversing; second, the unified subjectivity across multiple subjectivities can be understood as an occasion by which the collection of subjects is increased by one and not reduced to one; Whitehead's "…and increased by one.").

Merleau-Ponty (1964/1968) provides another charmingly simple do-it-yourself-experiment that demonstrates the many consciousnesses that the human subject entertains at any given moment. This time there is only a single instruction: take hold of any object that is sufficient enough that it may be grasped with both hands. Given my current environment, I am finding it exceedingly difficult to avoid the object of the computer's keyboard. For the reader, this might be the discrete objective totality of these pages, however they have been bound. Consider the keyboard. My fingertips rest on an expanse of keys that are homogenous to the touch but heterogenous in capacity. However, it is but one keyboard. I have *two* hands, they survey a *single* keyboard and do so with a *single* objective. Fingers are not tasked with the responsibility of a few keys each; they come together indiscriminately to type the words I have in mind. Were I to break my right index finger, I wouldn't end up with a bunch of gaps in the words whenever an "h," "j," "y," and so on would otherwise be found. These would be absorbed by one of the adjacent fingers because all of the fingers are unified in the single text-producing activity. With an intact corpus collosum, I do not know what it would be like to engineer two papers simultaneously—one tasked to the right hand and the other tasked to the left. Given the apparent bilateral collaboration, is this sufficient to suggest the mediation of *one* consciousness? Merleau-Ponty explains his analysis of this experiment:

> But for my two hands to open upon one sole world, it does not suffice that they
> be given to one sole consciousness—or if that were the case the difficulty
> before us would disappear: since other bodies would be known by me in the

same way as would be my own, they and I would still be dealing with the same world. (p. 141)

Here Merleau-Ponty refers to a previous example he had already supplied. When speaking aloud, the auditory experience of my own voice, muffled also through my sinuses, is far different from the auditory experience I have of the voice of another. It is even different than the auditory experience I have of my own voice when it has been played back for me. In each case, something must be said for this transformation—there must be more than one single consciousness responsible for the integration of sense-data. He continues,

> If nonetheless they have to do with one sole tangible, it is because there exists a very peculiar relation from one to the other, across the corporeal space—like that holding between my two eyes—making of my hands one sole organ of experience, as it makes of my two eyes the channels of one sole Cyclopean vision. [...] [T]hese little subjectivities [...] could be assembled like flowers into a bouquet, when each being "consciousness of," being For Itself, reduces the others into objects. We will get out of the difficulty only be renouncing the bifurcation of the "consciousness of" the object, by admitting that my synergetic body is not an object, that it assembles into a cluster the "consciousnesses" adherent to its hands, to its eyes, by an operation that is in relation to them later, transversal; that "my consciousness" is not the synthetic, uncreated, centrifugal unity of a multitude of "consciousnesses of..." which would be centrifugal like it is, that it is sustained, subtended, by the prereflective and preobjective unity of my body. (pp. 141-142)

The unification between the object as experienced through the right hand with that through the left is less of a *single subjectification* than it is conciliation between *two subjectifications*. Each hand represents an intentional consciousness—a *being-towards* book, keyboard, or plastic c-4 explosives. These subjectifications, these "consciousnesses of..." are collected together into a bouquet of experience.

In his *Phenomenology of Perception*, Merleau-Ponty attributes this bouquet to a single, primordial consciousness. This is where the subject is practically deified—as if only the human subject is capable of commanding this process of unification. This is where twentieth century thinking has gotten locked in. It is why he explains that "The problems posed in *Ph.P.* are insoluble because I start there from the 'consciousness'-'object' distinction" (p. 200). Following Whitehead, he begins to wonder if he cannot suspend the assumed centrality of human consciousness, and instead begin to recognize unifying processes as orchestrated by consciousnesses—like the fingers on a keyboard. If this primordial, super-natural consciousness is suspended, then the unified object as touched by the right and left hands will begin to emerge as distinct "consciousnesses of..." that nevertheless find cohesion. To the ranks of subjectivities, the unified version of human subjectivity is added.

Instead of being left with a definite consciousness and a definite object-of-consciousness, one finds a singular occasion of becoming through which the roles previously played—subject, object, independent entity, etc.—continually perish and from which new roles are played, and so on. All of this may be seen without leaving the human subject. Merleau-Ponty explains that this may be extended to nature writ large:

> If one wants metaphors, it would be better to say that the body sensed and the body sentient are as the obverse and the reverse, or again, as two segments of one sole circular course which goes above from left to right and below from right to left, but which is but one sole movement in its two phases. And everything said about the sensed body pertains to the whole of the sensible of which it is a part, and to the world. (p. 138)

## Moving beyond the Orthodox Human Subject

Merleau-Ponty has done well to show that it is not necessary to assume an imperial subject: a subject whose command was originally thought to order the world. Indeed, doing so puts this subject (consciousness, language) over and above nature. But by keeping the subject as a part *of* nature allows a single language, applicable to nature in its multiplicity. This has been demonstrated in the act of perception in two ways. First, Merleau-Ponty has demonstrated how the roles of subject and object are always on the verge of reversing; second, the unified subjectivity across subjectivities can be understood as an occasion by which the collection of subjects are increased by one and not reduced to one.

If it is accepted that subjectivity applies not only to one's unified and embodied consciousness but may also apply to the various appendages of sense-perception, then perhaps the notion of subjectivity can leave behind the human entirely. Merleau-Ponty suggests that the reversibility of *flesh* even requires this extension.

> Through this crisscrossing within it of the touching and the tangible, its own movements incorporate themselves into the universe they interrogate, are recorded on the same map as it; the two systems are applied upon one another, as the two halves of an orange. (p. 133)

By limiting the role of subjectivity to the human observer (and her appendages), then the reversibility between human and nature would be impossible. Once again, this places the human over and above nature—a position that Merleau-Ponty has taken great care to avoid. Though bifurcated, nature does not hierarchize its constituent entities: all are included and, moreover, each entity fits equally well into the categories supplied by nature's historical bifurcation. "Since the same body sees and touches, visible and tangible belong to the same world" (p. 134).

It is not necessary to limit the event of flesh to human subjects. White-head and Merleau-Ponty may both be found expanding the notion of subjec-tivity to include nonhumans. However, there is a great deal of work left to be done. Some of this has already been started: the arguments for the subjectiv-ity, phenomenology, and psychology of nonhuman entities has been taken up within the humanities and have proceeded at the level of philosophical spec-ulation. This means that the tools have not yet been developed to empirically investigate the human subject as a nonanthropomorphic subject. The impact that these projects have on humanistic psychology will be examined in what follows.

The first step for doing so is to get rid of the anthropocentric "self" of psychology. Whitehead finds that his extensive training in mathematics sup-plies the method necessary for doing so. He explains how in mathematical studies, it is sometimes necessary to get rid of variables that are irrelevant for solving the problem at hand. The same step may be taken in order to get past the anthropocentrism implicit in the psychological self. "Let us therefore give a general description of this personal unity by divesting it of minor details of humanity" (p. 187).

The very definiteness of a human self, if maintained, makes Merleau-Ponty's reversibility impossible. In order for the objects that one touches to reverse roles with the subject, it must be maintained that such objects partici-pate equally in the creation of the constellation of individuality or the becom-ing of an individual. This would mean that the elevation profile, composition, and maintenance of the trails as well as the temperature and weather are just as responsible for my habits as a trail runner as I am. Moreover, my running on a given trail is, in part, responsible for the trails identity as a trail, for example by contributing to the lack of growth over the areas I step, and clearing the brush that smacks me in the face as I move through it.

By arguing that only humans may enjoy the self-organizing features of individuality, one places said humans over and above nature. Instead, hu-mans and their identities must be considered as part *of* nature. Self-ing is occurring all of the time. It is worth mentioning here that American clinical psychologist Randy Moss has argued for the benefits of a dynamic or fluid self within the context of therapy. As indicated in the neo-Freudian psycho-therapeutic tradition, and certainly through the social-critical trends, the self considered as a static and unchanging collection of biographical details is a problematic assumption that is responsible for many restricted capacities for being. Using Whitehead, Moss has encouraged clients to begin looking at their identities less as sedimented actualities and more as processes that are continually coming about and passing away.

## Subjectless Subjectivity

Since "subjectivity" has a long tradition of being a uniquely human role, the reference to nonhuman subjects has been called "subjectless subjectivity" (Bains, 2002). By shedding the privilege or exclusivity of human subjectivity in order to consider subjectless subjectivities, the problem of anthropocentrism dissipates. However, one is not yet prepared to proceed. The next problem that emerges is that of anthropomorphism. This is the assumption that smart-phones, cocker-spaniels, and pyrite all interact with the world with affectual relations similar to those of humans. It must again be stated that the argument for a non-anthropomorphic and non-anthropocentric subjectivity remains at the level of theoretical speculation. It is not sufficient to attribute human concern to the subjectivity of nonhuman things. Merleau-Ponty instead suggests that the key to understanding is through ontogenesis—of which the body is an example. If ontogenesis is the becoming of ontic substances through dynamic subjectification, then autopoiesis can be understood as the becoming of an individuality (consciousness, self, subject). Bains (2002) explains,

> [A] definition of autonomy or autopoiesis distinguishes itself from any purely thermodynamic definition that is solely constituted by relational flows. An autopoietic event has an endo-consistency that is lacking in a vortex or dissipative structure defined only by its relational flows with the surrounding medium. A baby or a molecule or a paramecium is not in and of itself a whirlpool or vortex or a wave or a crystal although it involves dissipative structures and can display vortex-like 'behavior.' It is a sovereign individual autonomy with an intrinsic existential reality or self-referential territory, even though it has relations with other existential territories. It is a value that is an end in itself—for its own sake. Very few philosophers [...] have attempted to think the possibility of an existential integrity that is at the same time in relation with other self-referential territories or events. (pp. 102-13)

Indeed, Bains has considered fetuses, molecules, and paramecia without recourse to anthropomorphism or anthropocentrism. Furthermore, each demonstrates what could be understood as a unique autopoeitic process—complete with relations to other territories and a unique and distinct existential integrity. This does not, however, mean that shoelaces, lampshades, and miracle grow must constantly review themselves as if by way of a mirror—this type of conscious self-reflexivity is not what is meant by subjectivity. A subject need not recognize its singularity and autonomy as subject. That is, a subject need not be conscious of its subjectivity. Now we must add "consciousness" to Whitehead's garbage pail of discarded details.

## Intentional Unconscious

In developing the language with which to discuss nature in its many forms, we have found it necessary to momentarily shed the detail of the human. This is because subjectivity has traditionally been reserved for the human subject. However, Merleau-Ponty's discussion of *flesh* suggests that the reversibility that one experiences as a subject-object must also extend to the objects one prehends. By refusing to extend reversibility to nonhuman objects, one necessarily places humanity over and above nature. Once again, this is precisely what is trying to be avoided in the present project. After migrating across the chasm from human subjectivity to nonhuman subjectivity, termed "subject-less subjectivity" above—all the while careful not to fall into the trap of anthropomorphism—the first problem that arises is the assumption that subjectivity must be self-conscious. Returning again to the anthropocentrically self-conscious human, the notions of consciousness and self-consciousness must be dealt with. Phenomenology has kidnapped consciousness and chained it forever to the intentional human. In order to free consciousness from this usage, it must lose its primacy through which it has held intentional sway over the universe (Sparrow, 2014). *Un*consciousness—the non-self-reflective and nonanthropomorphic notion of subjective prehension that applies to humans as well as humvees—will instead be considered primary. This, Bains (2002) observes, is contrary to the more typical correlationist discussions of subjectivity where consciousness is concerned:

> This phenomenological subjectivity is characterized by a particular (bizarre) understanding of visual perception and does not envisage the possibility of a subjectivity [...] that does not operate in the mode of phenomenology's understanding of visual perception but is rather a direct non-discursive auto-possession—a non-human for-itself. (p. 105)

By giving up the uniquely human, self-reflective consciousness—subtracting this capacity even from the human—one risks losing privileged capacities such as will, intention, and agency. This is why "consciousness" has been momentarily replaced with "unconsciousness." The latter is less-likely to carry with it the baggage of the recently mentioned privileged human capacities. As soon as consciousness loses its super-natural privilege, it may once again be used to describe the process of folding a necktie into a full-Windsor.

Canadian cognitive neuroscientist Brian Massumi (1995) tells a story that will help us begin to "shed the detail" of super-natural human consciousness. It is a description of Libet's (1985) experiment that demonstrates that intentional action actually *precedes* intentional desire, will, logic, and any form of self-referentiality. He explains,

Brain waves of healthy volunteers were monitored by an electroencephalo-graph (EEG) machine. The subjects were asked to flex a finger at a moment of their choosing, and to note the time of their decision on a clock. The flexes came 0.2 seconds after they clocked the decision. But the EEG machine regis-tered significant brain activity 0.3 seconds before the decision. (p. 90)

For which Massumi provides the following commentary,

It should be noted in particular that during the mysterious half-second [be-tween brain function and response], what we think of as "higher" functions, such as volition, are apparently being performed by autonomic, bodily reac-tions occurring in the brain but outside consciousness, and between brain and finger, but prior to action and expression. (p. 90)

It seems as though this privileged, ontologically primary access to the world—that is, super-natural consciousness—actually follows the actions it is said to facilitate. In returning to the previous problem presented by the non-self-reflective subjectivity of my shoelaces: if self-reflection is the stick-ing point necessary for subjectivity to hold, then it seems that human subjects also fall short. Of course this is only until consciousness loses its super-Natural privilege and ontological primacy. Instead of maintaining the corre-lationist assumption that consciousness is a uniquely human phenomenon, Bains has found insight from the French philosopher of biology, Raymond Ruyer (1902-1987). Ruyer (1966) explains the difficulty in considering a subjectless subjectivity:

"But it is very difficult, in spite of oneself, to not be led to think that a being that is conscious of its own form represents a more mysterious type of con-sciousness than a being that is conscious, through modulations of sensory information, of the form of exterior objects. It is very difficult to admit that a protoplasm, a molecular edifice, and embryo, an organic tissue or a cortex, are conscious of themselves (possess their own form) before becoming, by added modulation, conscious of the form of other beings, and without being obliged to pass by this detour. (p. 167; in Bains, 2002, p. 113).

To be sure, considering the consciousness of thumbtacks or particle boards challenges the limits of comfortably orthodox philosophical thought. Howev-er, the philosophers that have been engaged throughout this chapter give no indication that comfort or orthodoxy is in any way guaranteed. Indeed, a faithful commitment to their insights requires an expansion of the traditional notion of subjectivity. Merleau-Ponty's concepts of flesh and reversibility allow for a complicated subject-object interrelationship that avoids their cor-relationist collapse into human subject; Whitehead's concept of prehension provides a language of intentionality that applies equally well to subjects and objects, allowing for the flexibility in these terms required by their reversibility.

## NOTE

1. Reversibility is a quality of nature. As it stands, however, the subject-object reversibility may only be demonstrated through the human sub-objective event. This is because humans may be explored as an object and as a subject, whereas the investigation of other entities in nature are limited to objective procedures. The possibility of a phenomenology of nonhuman entities is explored in the following chapter, but it remains at the level of recognizing reciprocal transformations that occur within and across entities from a phenomenological vantage point. It does not begin with gathering phenomenological data.

*Chapter Six*

# Problem Three

## *Rejecting Posthuman Possibilities*

The third problem that I would like to describe concerns the humanistic assumption that there are certain limits put in place that constitutes the human. This is because any such definition of human must locate itself within a particular historical, political, and cultural context. For humanistic psychologists, this context was the middle of this past century. In the 1940s and 1950s, particular in the psychology laboratories of the United States, it had become customary to reduce human beings to finite repertoires of behaviors, and discrete systems of biological function. Humanistic psychologists resisted these practices, arguing instead for a psychology that focuses on the whole human (without reducing her to smaller parts). Psychology, they argued, should focus on *human* concerns, and they began exploring the world of human experience.

In the decades that followed, this world of the human began to change through technologies of connectivity (among others). Telephones began appearing in every household, then computers, then the internet, and finally mobile devices that have evolved rapidly in the last fifteen years (see below). As the use of, and dependence on, technology began to grow, the human beings that used them began to change in the direction of this technology. For example, the speed with which information is available through the internet has transformed the patience I have as a researcher for finding a particular book or journal article when I learn about it. Even ten years ago I would have to drive to the university library, check the listings (which had just been updated from note-card to digital), and then request that a copy be mailed to the library for my pick-up sometimes weeks later. Today, if I cannot find a digital copy of the text immediately, I can request it and have it mailed

directly to me all from the comfort of my home. This impatience for information is not human—I have learned it from the technology that has transformed the availability and accessibility of information. This new attribute of
being a researcher in the twenty-first century is a posthuman attribute, because it expands the human being in the direction of technological development. The world of human experience that humanistic psychologists began
exploring in the 1960s has grown. However, rather than expand the exploration to include these important changes, there has been a *de facto* rejection of
any transformation of the human that does not resemble the ideal form of the
1960s human. Humanistic psychologists continue to insist that the best human relationships are the ones that took place in the 1960s—the ones that
had not yet been mediated by Twitter, Snapchat, and Facebook.

In this chapter, I argue that by continuing to reject posthuman possibilities, humanistic psychologists are in violation of the humanistic axiom of
fidelity to the subject. They do not allow that human experience may be
transformed by technology without judging it as unfortunate. This is a problem because it invalidates human experience, something that humanistic
psychologists have advocated against since the beginning. However, all that
must be done to avoid this violation is to expand what it means to be a
human—that is, recognize and accept that humankind has changed over the
last sixty years. More specifically, humankind has changed in the direction of
technology. Once this is accepted, inquiry may continue as usual by looking
to the human subject for an understanding of the increasingly posthuman
world.

## MODERN AND HUMANISTIC CONCEPTIONS
## OF SOCIAL MEDIA

Computer- and internet-mediated social networks must first be situated within the modernist and humanist conceptions of nature that have characterized
contemporary scientific practice. This distinction has been proposed by Merleau-Ponty in his course-notes on *Nature* (1956-57/2003). Modernism may
be understood as the practice of science indicated in Whitehead (1925/1953,
1929/1978) and Husserl (1931/2002, 1970), which operates within an increasingly limited logical-empirical scope of mechanisticity and material reductionism. Humanism may be understood as the mid-century response to
these increasingly mechanistic modern sensibilities and instead privileges the
role of the human subject (e.g., Heidegger 1927/1962; Merleau-Ponty 1942/
1963, 1945/1962). It will be argued that neither of these models is sufficient
for understanding the increasingly complicated role played by social technology in the lives of humans. Modernists maintain that technology may be used
to the benefit of human sociality, and that this influence is unidirectional;

modernists also claim that this is a good thing. Humanists maintain that the technology has not only shaped human sociality, but has begun to transform the humans themselves. Moreover, since this has changed human being, humanists claim that this is a bad thing. Both conceptions of the relationship between social technology and its users have placed humans over and above nature. As such, the possibilities that evolving social technology yields are passed over.

## Modernist View of Social Media

Viewed as a closed mechanical system, modernists understand social networking as a specifically human technology that can be used by humans for definite, if limited purposes. For example, as a helpful technology, social networking can be understood as an extension of one's social surface area for enhanced sociality (a metaphor that has been appropriately borrowed from the world of geometry). Given modernist assumptions, the differences between persons who are plugged into social media and those who are not may be limited to terms of social surface-area: the former enjoys one that is far more broad and connected. Turkle (2012) observes that her colleagues in the MIT Department of Computer Science regard social networking in this capacity. However, it should be noted that Turkle, an avowed humanist, does not share their enthusiasm.

## Humanistic View of Social Media

The humanists refuse to allow the modernists such a clean unidirectional relationship between social media and its users. The former is not *merely* an additive to the latter. Instead, there is a far more sophisticated reciprocal relationship between social media and its user—the latter shapes the former and the former, the latter. Given the consequences of the bidirectional relationship between humans and technology, humanists wring their hands with indignation at the *inhumanity* thus wrought. Here Turkle (2012) is found waving the caution-flag as society begins to transition away from primary, human interaction and toward secondary, computer-mediated interaction. She maintains that the latter is in principle an impoverished form of the former. Jaron Lanier (2009) similarly decries the slow but noticeable shift away from personal relationships. He observes that individuals and their relationships have been transformed by arbitrary social media program-design, and that this is a problem. In his analysis, Lanier combines phenomenology with his professional interest in virtual reality in order to demonstrate precisely how these transformations have come about. In sum, humanists understand a sophisticated bidirectional relationship between social media and the humans that use them. Given their principled veneration of humanity, humanists are understandably mortified by the slow "dehumanization" at work.

Turkle (2012) nicely summarizes the deficiency of a modernist conception of social media by demonstrating the sophisticated relationship between technology and its user:

> While my computer science colleagues were immersed in getting computers to do ingenious things, I had other concerns. How were computers changing us as people? My colleagues often objected, insisting that computers were "just tools." But I was certain that the "just" in that sentence was deceiving. We are shaped by our tools. And now, the computer, a machine on the border of becoming a mind, was changing and shaping us. (p. x)

Consistent with the modernist conception of nature, Turkle's colleagues at MIT assume that technology may be created, shaped, and transformed by humans and in service to humans. For the modernist, the sky is the limit for what technology might be able to do for humans. But Turkle observes that the relationship between technology and human is not so simple, and that it is certainly not unidirectional. Indeed, technology is not the only participant in the relationship that is undergoing change—humans are changing too. She writes,

> We make our technologies, and they, in turn, shape us. So, of every technology we must ask, Does it serve our human purposes?—a question that causes us to reconsider what these purposes are. Technologies, in every generation, present opportunities to reflect on our values and direction. (p. 19)

By demonstrating a reciprocal relationship between humans and technologies, the humanist conception of nature already far exceeds the complexity of the modernist model. Technology does not serve a limited purpose, but participates in the transformation of the human-technology relationship. This sophisticated system of interconnection recognizes a new and more expanded range of possibility. Her concluding question as to the usefulness of technology for specifically human purposes will be taken up later.

## Modernism and Humanism Both Place Humans Outside of Nature

Each of these conceptions of nature—modern and humanistic—have managed to place the human outside of nature. This can be demonstrated by the ways in which social technology has been positioned. The modern view maintains social media is a useful tool with definite, albeit limited advantages. This tool can be used to extend one's sociality: expanding the network of individuals with which one can socially engage, cross-referencing individuals in order to identify particularly appealing personality traits, or eliminating proximity constraints from social interaction. In each of these cases, humans benefit by manipulating certain factors, or employing certain tools in order to improve social conditions. These tools otherwise remain inert and benign. Through corrections to existing social technology and the production of newer forms, modernists anticipate a steady improvement of human-access to this sociality-thing through time. One finds that humans and sociality have been ontologically divided and it is the humans who are doing the active manipulating. That humans socialize might be considered natural, but modernists place humans over and above this natural process by the assumption that sociality can be controllably manipulated.

Like the modernists, humanists might view sociality as a natural process. The humanists seem to view social media as a secondary better-than-nothing good. Turkle (2012) explains this position when she writes how "[o]nline connections were first conceived as a substitute for face-to-face contact when the latter was for some reason impractical" (p. 13). That is, the human interaction mediated by shared physical proximity is the best; skipping to the introduction of social technology, video-conferencing, which combines the sound and sight of the *real thing,* might be next; this would be followed by telephone; and again by texts and emails, etc. Here one finds a hierarchy of social-connectivity that places the untechnologically-mediated human-human interaction at the top. Since I cannot reasonably meet face to face with my sister who lives two-thousand miles away, I can opt for the next-best thing and call her for free with Skype, which allows nearly-real-time video-talking. This latter option would only be appropriate provided the former was inconceivable. Indeed, something is better than nothing. As such, humanists cautiously condone the use of social technology, always quick to remind its users that it is an impoverished form of the *real thing.* By suggesting that the social interactions mediated by technology necessarily limit an otherwise natural process, humanists not only place technology outside of nature, but also find these events to be in opposition. While humanists might count themselves among the ranks of nature, anthropocentric privileging suggests that humans stand over and above nature. Like technology, humanists view nature as something *for* them, and not merely something of which they are a part.

## The Humanistic Anti-technology Polemic: Rejecting the Posthuman

Upon reviewing her forty years of investigation into the increasing role played by technology in the social world, Sherry Turkle (2012) shares her concern about the direction of this trend. Turkle does not concede to the modernist observations of her colleagues at MIT that the relationship between humans and technology is merely unidirectional—where the technology serves humanity. Adopting the humanistic stance, Turkle observes that the relationship is more complicated. Indeed, technology has begun to shape its human users. While this could be an exciting time to witness the evolution of humanity—a time during which the line between robots and humans gets blurred (as Mazis, 2008, has argued)—Turkle protests against this, drawing a line between human and machine while arguing that the latter is always an impoverished form of the former. Moreover, this humanistic assumption is used to discount the subjective reports of elderly persons who experience intimacy with pet robots, the adolescent claims that texting is preferable to talking, and the human clients who experience empathy from computer programs. In sum, adherence to humanistic assumptions denies the possibility of continued human evolution—as if humanity in the 1960s had reached some sort of apex. Moreover, it results in the dismissing of validity from subjective reports—an objection that humanistic psychologists have routinely raised against the practice of objective data collection.

Throughout her investigation of the now-complicated human-technology-system, Sherry Turkle (2012) repeatedly asks the question: "So, of every technology we must ask, Does it serve our human purposes?" (p. 19). She implies that technology can either serve human purposes or that it might otherwise be destructive to these purposes. Turkle indicates that humans are marked by real empathy and not the fake "as if" empathy, existential finitude and not the fake "as if" existential finitude, and real biological birth and not fake "as if" birth. She proposes the series of "as if" performances because the past three decades have been witness to increasingly sophisticated robots that are capable of demonstrating compelling versions of each of these. What is important is that Turkle is identifying differences between the normal human repertoire of experiences and the technologically mediated "as if" experiences. *The problematic humanist assumption here is that the "as if" version is in principle distinct from and deficient to the "normal".*

For example, psychotherapy programs (e.g., ELIZA; Weizenbaum, 1966) developed sixty years ago have "deceived" patients into false experiences of empathic intimacy. That is, human patients report the experience of being understood by programmed responses on a computer-screen. Turkle explains how this happens:

> Faced with a program that makes the smallest gesture suggesting it can empathize, people want to say something true. I have watched hundreds of people type a first sentence into the primitive ELIZA program. ... But four or five interchanges later, many are on to "My girlfriend left me," "I am worried that I might fail organic chemistry," or "My sister died." (p. 23)

Not only is empathy denied to computer programs, but the empathy that patients experience through computer programs is understood as being of a lesser form. Furthermore, these "as if" experiences are discerned from the real psychotherapy interactions. Despite the variability of empathic awareness within and across therapists, these forms are all preferable to the "as if" forms. That is, the real thing—defined in advance of the actual therapeutic interaction—is preferable to the "as if" thing.

The same may be said of the "as if" experiences of existentiality as reported by interacting humans. Turkle explains how singular individuality, typically reserved for human persons, is now being extended to robotic persons. In the nineties, it became popular for children to carry around little keychain eggs with a digital personality (called Tamagotchis). The electronic children would have to be taken care of—fed, cleaned up, put to bed, and so on. Ill or neglectful treatment would result in death at which point the program could be reset, replaced with an identical infant once more. However, instead of trying the experiment again, Turkle notes how such Tamagotchi deaths were followed by genuine remorse. That is to say—the children suffer existential guilt from resetting the digital personality!

Over the period of about twenty years, robots and computer programs have been increasingly characterized as having the kinds of interpersonal, emotional, and existential boundaries typically reserved for humans. Even Turkle herself admits having had this experience: "I did not anticipate how bad I would feel when [my Tamagotchi] died. I immediately hit the reset button. Somewhat to my surprise, I had no desire to take care of the new infant Tamagotchi that appeared on my screen" (p. 33). Yet she maintains throughout her study that "[t]he attachments I describe do not follow from whether computational objects really have emotion or intelligence, because they do not" (p. 20). The assumption here is that the elderly widow that suffers from loneliness would be better off with real human contact than with fake human contact—the kind provided by a robot or pet (or robot pet). Indeed, the experience of affection that transpires between human and robot is assumed to be an impoverished form of the real thing. Could it not be the opposite? Perhaps humans would be better off if disabused from the company of their human neighbors. While this notion is difficult to entertain, consider a less absurd version: communication. The classically humanistic assumption is that there is a difference in authenticity between direct human-human communication and those mediated by computers and technology.

While the examples thus far have illustrated the differences between human-human relationships and human-robot/program relationships, consider the human-human relationships that are mediated by technology. Once again one finds the classic humanistic assumption that the greater the degree of separation between the humans in a human-human relationship, the more impoverished version of communication that follows. While a telephone conversation is better than nothing, it must always be understood that it is an impoverished form of the real thing. Turkle shares the story of a young American woman named Ellen who had been working abroad for several years. Ellen had regularly called her grandmother long distance and was pleased when the technology came about that allowed her to video-call for free. Despite the fulfillment that her grandmother experienced, Ellen explained that her virtual presence was deceptive because she used the time to multitask on the computer. Turkle concludes, "Ellen and her grandmother were more connected than they had ever been before, but at the same time, each was 'alone'" (p. 14). Rather than reconcile her guilt at her disinterest in speaking with her grandmother, this is projected onto the medium for communication. It is as if she would not be distracted by her smart phone if she was in the same room with her grandmother, or she would not resent her grandmother for the drain to her productivity. The aloneness that Ellen and her grandmother experience is how the reader is to understand Turkle's title, *Alone Together*. Humans are increasingly connected to one-another—they are increasingly together, but since this connectivity is mediated by technology, it is marked by an unavoidable loneliness.

But the reversal could also be true. Though I am alone in my apartment and my mother alone in her house eight hundred miles away, we can still be together on the telephone. Though Levi Bryant, Nick Srnicek, and Graham Harman have never met in person, they were able to collaborate in editing a book (Bryant et al, 2011). While the togetherness that is mediated by a coffee-table or office-table is certainly different than the togetherness mediated by forms of cyber-technology, must one in principle be privileged over the other? Each event yields a multiplicity of possibilities as well as limitations, and each may be appreciated in its own right. However, by privileging the traditionally human over and above the technologically-mediated-human, Humanists restrict ontological depth of being to humans only.

## Silver-lining: Humanists Recognize the Evolution of Being

By suspending the privilege given to the traditionally human modes of interacting, the sophisticated systems of interconnectivity and reciprocal transformation may be used to expand the notions of traditionally human capacities. That is, their models of Nature expand the possibilities of the human-technology interaction. Traditionally, this has only been done up to a certain point: transformation is possible provided it "serves human purposes" or is not participant to dehumanization. However, were humanists to suspend the human-privilege and extend the capacity for reciprocal transformation even to the notions concerning human being, suddenly the dissolving boundaries between humans and technology are met with wonder and excitement instead of distress.

Turkle (2012) has observed the manner by which questions of life, existence, and being have transformed over the past forty years. These are proposed as examples of how technology has changed human expectations about humanity. This, Turkle argues, amounts to a dehumanization. For example, she summarizes her project with "a point of disturbing symmetry: we seem determined to give human qualities to objects and content to treat each other as things" (p. xiv). The reciprocal human-technology relationship has resulted in a transformation of each, but having predetermined what counts for "human," Turkle finds this to be disturbing. However, instead of looking at these instances of mutual transformation as disturbing, consider them instead as new possibilities of human being. Before moving into examples, consider the transformation that the traditional, 1960s "nuclear family" has undergone. Is this really to be understood as the high point of family dynamics? Must one concede that loving an adopted child "as if" he or she was one's own is an impoverished form of real parenthood? Or, moving closer to the present discussion—loving a Labrador retriever "as if" she were a child. Indeed, there is room for expansion and growth regarding the once-limited familial relationships. So too is there room for expansion and growth regarding human-technology relationships as well as technologically mediated relationships.

Over the years, Turkle has observed how "computers... turned children into philosophers." She continues, "In the presence of their simple electronic games... children asked if computers were alive, if they had different ways of thinking from people, and what, in the age of smart machines, was special about being a person" (p. x). Indeed, this question is becoming increasingly relevant in psychology, and it situates humanist brands of social science at a crossroads. Two options are available to the humanist social scientist. First, she can drive ontological stakes into the ground, standing for definite conceptions of human and acceptable methodological procedures, each based on an unchanging mid-century continental philosophy. That is to say that humanists can accept that they have become a 'normal' science complete with characteristic limitations in scope and maturity in methodological procedure. Second, she can maintain the spirit of creativity, daring, and expansion that has long been venerated in its tradition. This expansion extends to methodological procedures and would follow the continued evolution of the continental philosophies upon which it has been based; extends to the subject matter which is no less amenable to evolution; and it might even extend to the initial de facto rejection of alternative philosophies of science, finding the compassion even in Skinner (1972) and Watson (1930).

# Chapter Seven

# Recognizing How Technology Has Shaped Human Being

*Toward a Post-humanistic Psychology*

## THE PROJECTS OF POSTPHENOMENOLOGY

Every semester I have my general psychology students conduct a simple qualitative research project. I ask them to speculate about how technology has transformed the way we interact with one-another. Replacing the obligatory topic of social psychology, I have students develop a hypothesis about how technology has shaped the way that people interact socially. It could be how the limitations of text-messaging have added new words to our vocabulary like "LOL," "OMG," and "ROTFLMAO," or how video-conversations eliminate some of the barriers imposed by proximity constraints.

My goal with the midterm paper is fourfold: 1) have students develop a research question; 2) give students an opportunity to ask subjects their research question and record the responses; 3) use the responses to say something new about the original hypothesis; and 4) recognize how the technology that we use is changing us by the limitations it imposes and possibilities it provides for social interaction.

What's interesting is how supposedly terrible this transformation has been. "I remember a childhood where kids would hang out with and actually talk to one another instead of just staring at their cell phones," says the crotchety thirty-something, lamenting a bygone era of social intimacy. The assumption is that intimacy mediated by technology is necessarily a lesser form than human-human intimacy.

One student in particular reported deep shame in herself and her friends by describing how at a birthday party, seven or eight girls were all sitting around the restaurant table, eyes glued to their smart phones. Instead of interacting directly, these girls were taking pictures and posting them to a social media platform and interacting with the posts of one-another. The student woefully admitted "liking" the picture her friend, now seated across from her, had posted of the group just a few seconds earlier rather than telling her this to her face. So I asked her: "What was missing in the story you told?"

"Um… we weren't really interacting with one another."

But you were responding to one another's posts, and probably making it possible for several dozen others to interact as well.

"Yeah, but it's not the same as just talking."

Sure! Digitally mediated social interactions *are* different—that's correct. They both have their own sets of benefits and detriments. That's all. There is no reason to assume that digitally mediated interactions are, in principle, deficient to non-digitally-mediated interactions.

Without realizing it, I was asking my general psychology students to conduct their own rudimentary postphenomenological analyses. Following the phenomenological and digital humanities research of Don Ihde (1990; Rosenberger and Verbeek, 2015), postphenomenology recognizes that technology has been created by humans and has subsequently shaped what it means to be human.

By calling this area of digital humanities research *post*phenomenology, it recognizes that it has benefited tremendously from the groundwork laid by phenomenologists. Phenomenology is the continental school of philosophy that grew out of the early- to mid-twentieth century malaise regarding the material reductionism of experimentalism and logical empiricism in the nineteenth century. After decades of scientists reducing their subject matter to reflexes, machines, and smallest parts—biologists with their cells, physicists with their atoms, chemists with their elements, psychologists with their behaviors, and so on—the phenomenologists finally stood up and argued that the subject matter of science can never be so easily reduced without leaving something important out of the investigation. It is a position that is consonant with that of humanistic psychology that developed at around the same time.

Contrary to what Tom Sparrow argues in *The End of Phenomenology*, phenomenologists excel at *two* things. The first Sparrow agrees with: phenomenologists excel at rejecting the metaphysical position of modernity—the position that maintains that all processes may be understood by tiny pieces of matter bouncing into one-another based on fundamental axioms of physics. Sparrow maintains that the rejection of modern science is all the phenomenology has accomplished, and as such has failed to ever develop a method that might be useful for investigating experience, organic tissue, or ecosystems. Since he has already devoted several chapters to this rejection, I may move onto the second thing phenomenologists have excelled at: describing the reciprocal interactivity between self-regulating processes. This is precisely the act of intentionality: there are two individuals (in the physical, self-regulating and persistent sense of the term) that interact in an occasion of experience. Neither entity may give themselves entirely to an occasion of experience and will thus remain, to a certain degree, hidden. Husserl famously applied this to the perception of time; Merleau-Ponty to the perception of objects; and Levinas to the human-human interaction. But human experience is not the only place such an intertwining may be understood to occur— indeed, this intentional intertwining is the metaphysical platform to *replace* the modern model of mechanical physics (Rosen, 2008). Biologists Herbert Maturana and Francisco Varela (1972) famously applied such principles of reciprocal interactivity to their understanding of insects, organisms, and eventually the nervous system with what Varela would call neurophenomenology (1996).

Even still, the recognition that self-regulating entities interact in a reciprocal manner is not itself a method. Instead, it represents a shift in perspective. Once phenomenologists can get past the rejection of modern science, they may begin investigating the influence that entities share with one another. Postphenomenologists look at the relationship between humans and technology. Humans created technology; the technology has changed humans who in turn change the technology that in turn changes humans and so on. What emerges is a series of reciprocal influences that leave both forever changed and changing.

Postphenomenology also moves beyond the common playground of phenomenology because it looks specifically at how the human moves beyond herself. Merleau-Ponty, at least in his *Phenomenology of Perception*, has always kept phenomenology rooted in the human body: there was something fundamental about the "human body – world" connection. Martin Heidegger (2013) described an almost ethical obligation to avoid the pitfalls of technology. Like Mazis in chapter 3, postphenomenologists do not see any problems with "human – technology – world"; indeed, examining experience through its transformation by technology would be in fidelity to the subject. In their field guide to postphenomenology, Robert Rosenberger and Peter-Paul Verbeek (2015) explain that the heading expresses their ambivalence with respect to phenomenology:

> On the one hand, they are heavily inspired by the phenomenological emphasis on experience and concreteness, while on the other hand they distance themselves from the classical phenomenological romanticism regarding technology, and find a starting point in empirical analyses of actual technologies. (p. 9)

POSTPHENOMENOLOGICAL ANALYSES OF SMART PHONES

I became familiar with the professional work of Georgia Tech digital humanities professor Ian Bogost through his monographs he published through University of Minnesota Press's *Posthumanities* series. But to the nonacademic public, Bogost is famous for another reason: he developed a video game in order to demonstrate some of the economic and personal perils of mindless video games. It was called Cow Clicker. Players could click on a cow fifty times a day. If they wanted to click more than fifty times, they could purchase more clicks. The setup was asinine. But it became enormously successful—earning him more attention and popularity than anything else he had done in his career.

Bogost examines the relationship between humans and technology, with a particular interest in video games. But in 2015 he turned his focus to the fifth generation of apple's iPhone—a device that he metaphorically refers to as *The Geek's Chihuahua.* Like the toy dog that sits in a privileged place in your handbag, the iPhone forces the user to be patient, protective, thoughtful, ever-aware, and ultimately understanding of it. That is, instead of doing these things for us, the iPhone user must go extra lengths to look out for her iPhone. Hundreds of dollars are spent on cute cases and protective films or shields that mitigate the damaging effects of its being dropped on the ground—because even at $600, they are infinitely fragile. And if they're dropped, this is the user's fault, and not, for example, the developers' with the creation of a thin, nicely weighted slippery glass surface and plastic back. In his book, Bogost focuses on the myriad ways that the iPhone has transformed our daily experience. It has changed the way we stand in line at the grocery store, ride an elevator, eat breakfast, give directions, or wait for class to start. His analysis recognizes that this piece of technology has been powerfully influential, and devotes careful analytical attention to the concrete experience of its use. Though he did not adopt the term for his work, *The Geek's Chihuahua* is a postphenomenology of smart-phones—specifically the iPhone.

Galit Wellner performs an analysis similar to that of Bogost. But instead of looking at how one generation of smart phone has demanded that its users adapt to its unpredictable temperament, Wellner's analysis traces the shifts in cell phone technology over time. Beginning with the mid-nineties "brick" cell phone, she describes how cell phone features have shaped the behaviors, habits, and consciousness of their users. Wellner traces three important developments that occur from the portable brick cell-phone that could only make phone calls or send one-way, twenty-digit, numeric messages to the standard, internet-surfing, reciprocal-data-sharing smart phones (where, for example, information is shared between the user and the internet in real time and without any additional steps necessary—like an application that tracks heart rate, steps, and location and updates the user with pertinent health information, and so on). Each generation of cell phone imposes technologically relevant limitations on information sharing as well as interactivity between (and eventually, within) users. By understanding the important changes that have occurred through cellular phone technology over the last twenty years, Wellner is able to look forward into the future and speculate on the creative potential of new features of interactivity.

Postphenomenological analyses need not be relegated to the domain of cellular devices, but the latter come as easy examples for purposes of demonstration because they are so pervasive and their user-ship so broad. Postphenomenology examines the reciprocal interaction between humans and technology—recognizing that humans have created technology and technology has subsequently changed humanity (and on and on). The important detail that must always be observed is that humanity is not necessarily *better* or *worse off* because of transformations brought about by technology—humanity is only different; that is, humanity has been supplanted by posthumanity.

## ALIEN PHENOMENOLOGY: A SPECULATIVE METHODOLOGY FOR REALIST INQUIRY

Technology, the postphenomenologists argue, may be seen as an emanation of nature that can be explored through emergent posthuman methods of inquiry. Other branches of contemporary philosophy have been applying phenomenology in nontraditional ways as well. One particularly nonanthropocentric style is Bogost's *Alien Phenomenology.* Alien phenomenology considers the rapidly evolving world of social technology from a nonhuman vantage point. Bogost (2012), following the Object-oriented Ontology (OOO) of Graham Harman (2002/2006, 2005), argues that one *can* conduct a phenomenological investigation of nonhuman subjects. Bogost's *Alien Phenomenology* is a proposal for a nonanthropocentric and nonanthropomorphic phenomenological study of nature. His argument is that a non-human entity can be understood as a subjective-being-in-relation to other human or non-human entities. With his speculative method, Bogost tries to examine objects in a way that doesn't 1) reduce them to their significance for humans, and 2) doesn't anthropomorphize them with human likenesses. To view the world of objects in this way is to shed the significance of the human. Concrete slabs are flat and heavy, but what are some of their qualities that don't immediately translate into being-for-our-use? As a professor of digital humanities at Georgia Tech, Bogost has examined the ways in which technology has shaped people in posthuman ways—like how the various iterations of the iPhone have resulted in a variety of pathologies for the iPhone user (many of which the user is unaware).

Alien phenomenology considers the complicated interrelationships between objects by focusing on the particular capacities and limitations these objects provide. It is a method that follows the recent trend in continental philosophy called Speculative Realism (Bryant, Srnicek, and Harman, 2011). This trend promotes a sophisticated brand of realism that recognizes the limitations of nineteenth century forms of realism as they have been outlined by mid-century continental philosophers (e.g., Heidegger 1927/1962; Merleau-Ponty 1942/1963; Husserl 1970). Indeed, Speculative Realism is that which remains of realism after having undergone the transformation of phenomenology. Its inclusion of phenomenological insights allows for the complicated and dynamic processes of which objects and subjects are comprised. However, it does so without presupposing the starting point of the human subject. This is to say that objects might even be alien with respect to human relations, or that they exceed that which could be accounted for by human understanding.

Bogost observes a strong Western tradition of the placement of humans at the center of the universe in a manner reminiscent of geocentrism. Regarding the review of social media that has been summarized above, modernist and humanist conceptions equally situate humans in a position over and above nature—it is as if the latter exists only for the former. Bogost explains,

> The scientific process cares less for reality itself than it does for the discoverability of reality through human ingenuity. Likewise, the humanist doesn't believe in the world *except* as a structure erected in the interest of human culture. Like a mirror image of the scientist, the humanist mostly seeks to mine particular forms of culture, often by suggesting aspects of it that must be overcome through abstract notions of resistance or evolution. "Look at me!" shout both the scientist and the humanist. "Look what I have uncovered!" (p. 14)

By continuing investigation in this way, all objects maintain a seed of human-likeness. Bogost, following the dictates of Harman's (2002/2006) object-oriented ontology (OOO), has suggested alien phenomenology as a method that "puts *things* at the center of being." He continues, "[w]e humans are elements, but not the sole elements, of philosophical interest. OOO contends that nothing has special status, but that everything exists equally— plumbers, cotton, bonobos, DVD players, and sandstone, for example" (p. 6). Relationships of all sorts take the stage in alien phenomenology. That is, where traditional phenomenological investigations find the essence of things in their intentional relationship to consciousness, alien phenomenology expands this stricture to include other things as well. "In Whitehead's terms, it is a prehensive capability. In Husserl's terms, it is *noesis* divorced of consciousness, cogitation, intention, and other accidents of human reasoning" (p. 28).

Objects, now considered independently from humans, have what White-head (1933/1967) has termed "real potentiality." He explains that "[t]he 'potentiality' refers to a passive capacity," and "the term 'real' refers to the creative activity . . . " (p. 179). An object's passive capacity—that of which it is capable, taken together with its creative activity—its present ontological engagements, comprise its singular being-in-the-world. To investigate objects in their "real potentiality" requires an analysis of an object's current engagements in combination with speculation regarding its potential engagements. Bogost (2012) summarizes that "our job is to get our hands dirty with grease, juice, gunpowder, and gypsum. Our job is to go where *everyone* has gone before, but where few have bothered to linger. . . . I call this practice *alien phenomenology*" (p. 34).

In what follows, I want to share an alien postphenomenological analysis I performed with a friend of mine, Rustic Bowen, while we were in graduate school at the University of West Georiga. We took a careful look at Facebook's "Like" button. In the discussion, social media is used to demonstrate how technology has expanded the boundaries of what it means to be human.

## Alien Phenomenology and Social Media

Social media is an appropriate topic because it has been the focus of much debate between humanistically-minded psychologists and those who advocate a non-anthropocentric psychology. Social media refers to any technology that mediates human sociality. Though it was initially developed as a way of enhancing traditional social connectivity, e.g., by reducing barriers of proximity, there is considerable evidence that its implementation has shaped more than connectivity itself. Indeed, it has begun to shape its users (Lanier, 2009; Turkle, 2012). It is no longer humans who shape social media; this relationship is reciprocal. As such, social media will presently be considered as a non-human subject that is available to phenomenological investigation. It will explore social networking as an instance of "embodied technology"—that is, capable of dynamic interaction as intentional subjects (Mazis, 2008).

## Phenomenology and Embodied Technology

In order to recognize the interrelationship between humans and technology—unified above through an expanded notion of subjectivity supplied by Merleau-Ponty's flesh—the latter must first be freed from nineteenth century modernist laws of mechanisticity. "We think of matter as inert, as dumb, as senseless, and as self-contained. Yet what a strange predicament for a material being to fall into—to become closed off to the ongoing communication with other material beings!" (Mazis, 2008, p. 17). The twentieth century has freed the subject from the ontological abyss of ninteenth century objectivity, yet objects have been left at the level of lifeless, inert, and senseless matter. That is, subjects are free to engage the world in its multiplicity through reciprocal, mutually constitutional becomings; objects, however, remain where they were last put. Mazis (2008) uses phenomenology, primarily that of Merleau-Ponty (1942/1962; 1964/1968), to argue that objects have always participated in the dynamic forms of being—transformed by and transforming the world into which they are embedded. While this has always been the case, it has become increasingly apparent through the impressive evolution of technology.

Mazis (2008) maintains that the continued assumption that matter is uninvolved with its surroundings may be understood as carry-over from nineteenth century natural science. Mazis explains that it is this "dualistic, reflective perspective on bodies and materiality" that "short-circuit[s] attempts to think through the possible creative interpretations of the intertwining of human, animal, and machine" (pp. 14-15). This perspective has been powerfully challenged at the hands of phenomenology, yet this development has been limited to the being of humans. Human being is found engaged in reciprocal relationship to its surround—constituting its milieu and constituted by it. This engagement is mediated by the human body—Merleau-Ponty's "sensible sentient" (1964/1968). Thus human being, intelligence, ethics, etc., always come about by way of embodiment. This rhythmic, meaningful engagement is what makes humans more than nineteenth century mechanisms. Mazis (2008) demonstrates what happens when this logic is used to differentiate humans from machines. "Surely this is what makes the machine a 'mere object'—it has no relationship to its environment. Yet in our current era, machines are transforming and entering a more mature age of their development" (p. 49). Recognizing the role of embodiment in human intelligence means challenging Descartes' notion that rationality and intelligence exists independently of a body. It wasn't until this recognition was extended to machines that the latter were able to engage meaningfully and dynamically with the environment in a way that more closely resembles what is understood as human intelligence. Mazis describes the transformations that occur in artificial intelligence and robotics following the implementation of embodiment. As embodied technology, machines no longer passively react with preprogrammed responses to particular stimuli, but are free to *inter*act alongwith stimuli. By emphasizing the role of the body, what emerges is a dialogical relationship with the surrounding environment.

This dynamic and reciprocal embodied interaction with the environment is precisely what had been lacking in the development of artificial intelligence and machines in the 1980s. Deep Blue was a chess-playing computer program that was successful in defeating the World Champion. As a program, Deep Blue was capable of instantly calculating the probabilities of move selections across all available game scenarios. It existed as a complicated aggregate of unembodied yet perfectly rational propositions; Deep Blue was Descartes, self-actualized. Despite the ability to create a glorified rationalist philosopher, technologists and robotics-engineers had not yet been able to design a machine that was capable of buttering a piece of bread. Its computation brilliance was overshadowed by its profound limitations.

Embodied interaction with an environmental surrounding is a sophisticated form of intelligence that exceeds any quantity of rationalistic bits of information. Instead of looking for subjectivity or intelligence in an abstracted space of rationalistic form, these may be found within embodied interactions. This is not to say that subjectivity and intelligence are ideal forms; nor is it to say they are physical forms. Subjectivity and intelligence are demonstrated between entities through meaningfully engaged embodied interaction. Embodiment is the appropriate metaphor for advancing beyond the nineteenth century modernist notions of intelligence, and this must now be extended to objects (machines) as well.

> Traditionally, philosophers have thought of words, language, and writing as emanations of the human mind, but now many in differing fields realize that we should start thinking of how the materiality of language, words, writing, books, and a host of more literal information and perceptually related machines comprise the ways we think through our surround and the ways in which the surround comes to shape the way we think in the process. (p. 74)

## Hypernetworks Explode Human Conceptions of Reality

When looked at only through the veil of the twentieth century human, social networks are found playing an active role in the dehumanization of our relations with one another. These perspectives look to the past, lamenting that which we've lost. Speculative Realists, along with posthuman forms of inquiry, see nothing wrong with this transformation. In this final section, I would like to focus on how this transformation occurs through our use of social networks as well as a variety of internet information resources. I have selected Timothy Morton's 2013 analysis of *Hyperobjects* to help me do this. The hyperobject of social networking has challenged and fundamentally altered what it means to be human by obliterating the human reference points of space and time. Indeed, these have become increasingly impossible to speak of in human terms. Space, time, and the stuff found therein have become effectively social-network-morphized (and not anthropomorphized as the last three hundred years might have it). The hyperobject of social networks, which will now be referred to as the hypernetwork, has distributed itself throughout Earth with consequences that reverberate through the syntactical structures of written and spoken language, the conscientiousness of debilitating neurological diseases, and what it means to be visible, available, or attentive.

## What Is the Hypernetwork?

The hypernetwork is "massively distributed in time and space relative to humans" (Morton, p. 1). It humiliates human understanding by occupying unthinkable magnitudes of space, and by operating at incomprehensible speeds. This transforms the world it occupies—a statement that is intended ontologically and not phenomenologically. The unfathomable magnitudes of space and time—once understood to extend infinitely in all directions—are thrust upon the *here* and the *now.* This gives the impression that time and space are easily manageable. Take space for example. The sheer volume of events that occur within the Facebook platform is unimaginable. Facebook has more than one billion users (1.317). Every twenty minutes, 1 million links are added; 1.4 million event invitations are distributed, 1.9 million friend requests are accepted, 2.7 million photos are uploaded, 1.89 million statuses are updated, and 10.2 million comments are made (Caplan, 2013). Notice what happens to our sense of size and the spaces required to fit such quantities. These numbers land well outside of any meaningfully significant sense of number. Try to imagine what it means to stand in the physical presence of a billion people. This number could quite likely be reduced by 99.9 percent without any recognizable change. This number is unthinkably large; it is frighteningly large. Indeed, it can only be managed by the place-holder: "more than I can possibly imagine." Yet it has become perfectly normal to interact with and talk about such unimaginable things—with this unhuman scale. It is when the unimaginable becomes routine that we find ourselves at-home in a space that is entirely alien.

A similar transformation occurs regarding measures of time. The status updates that occur every twenty minutes, while unfathomably vast, seem to be able to occur without regard to friction or speed: it is as if they occur instantly. The user-load-bearing capability is so massive that it seems as though the 1.89 million status-updates can occur simultaneously. It is not that they occur without time, but that the slices by which we are wont to divide time are clunky and awkward relative to the hypernetwork. As a result, we begin to shave our units of time into smaller and smaller chunks, approaching the limit of instantaneous. I still wait many impatient moments—dozens even—while in line at the grocery store before advertising my disapproval. It only seems to occur as soon as my shopping cart comes to a halt because the division of human moments has been social-network-morphized—moments in which no human thing could possibly get done.

The Speculative Realist argument that I am advancing is that social networks have fundamentally transformed space and time by replacing the scales by which we understand them. Earth has taken on a twitterized likeness, even to the point of organizing itself into a haiku-esque parsing of characters. Moreover, there is no space left unperturbed.

## Where Must We Look for the Hypernetwork?

Morton explains how "we never see a hyperobject directly" (p. 153); we must infer it from the things it influences. We do not encounter the hypernetwork. Indeed, there is no ontic hypernetwork. The hypernetwork encounters us. Social networks are not taken advantage of by the humans that use them, but the reverse. Humans have become twitter-morphized, facebook-morphized, and instagram-morphized. The Earth has itself recalibrated: it has become effectively flattened and miniaturized by Google-Earth into a pocket-sized Pangaea—small enough to hold, but big enough for everyone and everything to hold it at the same time. This is not the same transformation that occurred through the creation and distribution of maps, because now you and I can zoom in on the same place, even "here." Moreover, we can both do so from the newest privileged vantage point: the aerial perspective (which I will talk about below).

The physical world no longer conforms to human limits of time and space. Whether this is something new, or merely something that has finally dawned on us is unclear. In any case, social networks make it evident. What happens right now will be captured in tweets and preserved with a twitter formaldehyde and left to be uncovered by some twenty-fourth century cyber-archaeological excavation. The tweets will also become immediately available across the globe. Twitter-morphized, this talk will occur everywhere and everywhen. Again, this is not to say that it is unbounded by time and space, but that time and space no longer carry themselves with the same human heft that they once did.

We see the hypernetwork in the still-frame Instagram-capturing of an event. It is not that an event or experience is fitted into an Instagram with the excess shaved off, but that the event gathers itself in this format. Serene sunsets and dangerous mountain-ranges orient themselves into 187,000 screen-savers—immortalizing themselves through the hypernetwork and thwarting ephemerality.

I will now look for the hypernetwork in the modifications it has made to space and time, though we will only have time for space—well, space for space. *A propos* of Speculative Realism, the hypernetwork shows little regard to anthropocentrism, upsetting the human scaling of the world. Space and time accordingly take on a social-network-likeness.

## What We Find

As we have begun to see, the hypernetwork has been at work slowly manipulating the physical relationships of things. Like the enormous sand-dunes along the coast of Lake Michigan that move steadily inland grain by grain, the hypernetwork has been slowly transforming space and time. A video showing the aftermath of a dentist-office-visit gets 126 million hits; a satellite camera captures a caribou stampede in Tuktut Nogait National Park from five hundred miles (eight hundred kilometers, eh?) above the Earth's surface; a 35,000-square-foot Facebook server-farm radiates heat to its surrounding environment (Facebook occupies space?!). These events chip away the human-scaling of time and space by obliterating our human points of reference. Regarding space, this may be seen in the collapsing of the unthinkable surface area of the Earth into a palm-sized map—where any featureless coordinate can be magnified down to a square meter. It is this new easily collapsible, easily navigable space with which we relate. Regarding time, the sheer speed by which tremendous volumes of processes can occur suggests that everything occurs without any temporal expenditure. Events no longer unfold gradually, but occur immediately (at least on a human scale). Let us look at space.

*Space.* Merleau-Ponty (1945/1962) provides an appropriate starting point for considering the transformation of space brought about by the hypernetwork. He explains how

> Space is not the setting (real or logical) in which things are arranged, but the means whereby the positing of things becomes possible. This means that instead of imagining it as a sort of ether in which all tings float, … we must think of it as the universal power enabling them to be connected. (p. 243)

The hypernetwork allows for connections in unhuman magnitudes, and we relate to these in their uncanny familiarity while our sense of space is modified. It is not that I have formerly enjoyed Tuktut Nogait National Park, or even that I know about someone who has, but I am able to explore it by satellite images and by reading about what few adventures have occurred there. That is, I can sift through the several hundred-thousand vacations that have taken place at National Parks that sit atop frozen tundra, and find one that looks appealing. I'll go "here." It is not that "there" has collapsed into "here," falling into my lap as it were—but this is how it seems. The scale by which distance is measured may be increased through a zooming function such that any distance seems inconsequential. Zoom out far enough and anything can be "right over there." It would be like trying to measure the length of my pant-inseam in miles: five ten-thousandths of a mile, when rounded to the nearest tenth, is zero. Everything is transported to here. I look at a map and say that I would like to go "here." I might even choose my own backyard. Not the backyard through my combination kitchen/laundry room, but the backyard I can locate and zoom in on: the backyard that is twelve minutes from campus, and one thousand miles from my hometown: each of these locations may be found within the same map if zoomed out far enough.

This relation to space invades those spaces we currently occupy, and the distinctly posthuman, aerial perspective seems to have been given unquestioned authority. It is as if the aerial image captured by satellite is Merleau-Ponty's fugitive image of the house seen from all perspectives at once. "Here" seems to have more to do with this new alien perspective than familiar human ones. This satellite-view has replaced curb-appeal or the human aesthetic associated with spaces. For example, *Telegraph* reporters (2013) in the UK write about how "Residents of a quiet housing estate twinned with a German town were shocked to find their homes are shaped—like a swastika. An aerial view of the dozen houses in Devizes, Wiltshire reveals they look just like Hitler's symbol" (November 17). Home-owners shrugged their shoulders, reasoning that it was too late to do anything now. The builders apparently had failed to consider the alien perspective when drawing up blueprints. In a more shocking example, *TIME* writers explain how the Coronado Naval Amphibious Base in San Diego stood for forty years before the aerial shots from Google Earth revealed that "four unconnected buildings on the base formed an unfortunate shape when viewed from above: a swastika." (http://content.time.com/time/specials/packages/article/0,28804,1881770_1881787_1881780,00.html). The Navy subsequently reported plans to spend $600,000 to mask the shape. And they have done so.

Physical space has become entirely coded in terms of proximity to hyper-network outlets: an isolated cabin is viewed as having a dangling, unconnected network cable. Its rustic backdrop replaces an urban or academic backdrop the way one might change their desktop background or Facebook cover-photo. Even the denizens of some fictitious unconnected island community are subject to the transformation of temporality and spatiality imposed upon them by the hypernetwork. Google Earth captures their terrain and transmits it immediately into a hundred-million homes. As such, these spaces appear as easily navigable as the international travel hubs like Atlanta, London, Beijing, or Dubai. Within the magnetic field of the hypernetwork, the world opens up as a flat, instantaneous, and local space.

## EXPANDED SUBJECTIVITY AND EMBODIED INTELLIGENCE

Each of the above examples demonstrate two things: 1) technology has changed what it means to be human and 2) it is still possible to investigate the human through these transformations. There is no reason that humanistic psychologists cannot continue their efforts to understand the subject in her or his world of experience. However, in order to do so requires that the 1960s notion of "human" be replaced by one that matches the experience of the twenty-first century human. The category must expand to include all human experiences—experiences that are becoming increasingly posthuman in nature.

Human-human social events represent just one among many types of social events, and more broadly, social events represent just one among many types of events. By considering the discrete mechanisms of media programs in terms of their capacity for embodied and situated engagement with their surrounding, modernists may bear witness to and even participate in nature's evolution in its social-technological iteration. For example, the created programs—due to programmer undersight or oversight—might begin to complete tasks they had not been designed to complete, or complete them in a nonhuman manner which opens up new possibilities. However, to say that modernists might thus expedite nature's evolution would be to fall out of nature's conciliation. By suspending the privileging of human-human social interaction over other, allegedly deficient and impoverished forms, humanists find that different or alternative modes of social interaction have different and alternative capacities that are no less or more real. However, to say that humans become the sole beneficiary of social evolution misses out on the benefits shared by tracking cookies, firmware, and birthday notifications. Considered in their investigation of conciliated nature, modernists and humanists—traditionally opposed—may be found mutually benefiting from alternative posthuman methodologies.

## Expanding the Notions of Subjectivity, Intelligence

To oversimplify the ontological presuppositions of the previously mentioned conceptions of nature, the modernist begins with objects while the humanist begins with subjects. Modern philosophy and its scientific practices followed Parmenides in the assumption that nature is a static entity, available to investigation. As a result, all dynamic processes were dropped from investigation. This is most evident in the edicts of the Vienna Circle that effectively eliminated "phenomenal" as a valid subject matter for the logical empirical scientist (Polkinghorne, 1982). In what amounts to a response to the preoccupation with objectivist epistemologies, humanist philosophy (e.g., mid-century continental philosophy; Heidegger 1927/1962; Merleau-Ponty 1942/1963; and Husserl 1970) and its scientific practices began to follow Heraclitus in the assumption that nature is a dynamic process in which subjects and objects co-participate. The strong suggestion across these complicated dynamic interrelationships is that they may be explored only though the human subject—hence Merleau-Ponty's (1956-60/2003) assignment of the term "human-ist" to designate this dynamic assumption about nature. Once more in simplified form, the modernist begins with objects while the humanist begins with subjects. Since the present discussion concerning social technology has shown that each of these conceptions of nature put humans outside of the human-technology relationship, these notions of subject and object must be expanded. This will allow these notions to be equally applicable to both technology *and* its user.

## Expanding Subjectivity to Include Technology

In modernist thought, subjectivity has been interpreted as the bogeyman through which error is introduced to experimentation; in humanist thought, subjectivity is understood as the single vehicle of experience and thus enjoys a monopoly on ontological validity. By expanding the concept of subjectivity, the goal is not to unify the modernist and humanist claims. Though two, these constitutive parts fold into one-another and overlap in what Merleau-Ponty (1964/1968) has called flesh. This overlapping between subject and object results in an intertwining such that the continued discussion of separation becomes increasingly impossible. Understood as flesh, subjects and objects are understood as distinct, but they overlap to such a degree that one eventually has trouble deciding to which side of the duality each part belongs. Indeed, it soon becomes understandable to speak of the subjectivity of objects, and the objectivity of subjects. Whitehead (1929/1978; 1933/1956) has introduced the term prehension to describe the subject-object relation in a way that privileges neither. This expands the population to whom subjectivity and consciousness applies. Subjectivity begins to leave behind the traditional (human) subject; consciousness begins to leave behind the traditionally conscious (human). For example, Merleau-Ponty (1964/1968) has proposed that consciousness need not be limited to a human totality, but may be understood as emanating from appendages or even tissue. Moreover, the question of objective or subjective identity must be raised. In expanding the notions of subjectivity, objectivity, consciousness, and sentience, it will be argued that the once exclusively human subject expands to include nature in its many manifestations. This will be followed by an emphasis on the technological or machinic body. Merleau-Ponty's (1945/1962) notion of embodied consciousness has been applied to technological design in was has been called embodied intelligence; this has allowed for a dynamic and reciprocal relationship between machine and its environmental surrounding (Mazis, 2008).

# Chapter Eight

# The Radical Edge

*Object-oriented Psychology or,*
*Toward a Psychology of Things*

After dissolving the ontological boundaries in-between inert matter, living organisms, and human beings, collapsing the epistemological categories of subjectivity and objectivity, and turning the processes and procedures of humanistic psychology toward the transformation of human being by technology, a novel opportunity presents itself: could there be a psychology of things—that is, things absent humans?

Speculative realism (Bryant, Srnicek, and Harman, 2011), defined in more detail in chapter 7, has turned the focus of transcendental philosophy from a focus on human consciousness to a focus on the world of objects. Doing so has resulted in a much different style of asking and answering questions. By changing the routines of philosophical and scientific inquiry, and in challenging assumptions and expectations, it is hoped that contemporary research will grow in insightful new ways—ways that may have been previously restricted by tradition.

By returning to the world of objects with rejuvenated interest, is it possible that there is a world there that was previously restricted to the realm of human being? Could there be a psychology of objects?

In order to understand the boundaries of psychology, Whitehead (1929/1978) maintains that it must be applied in diverse and unorthodox ways. That is, in order to understand the importance that psychology might have for the world of physics, for example, it must be applied to the world of physics. Stapp (2011) provides one such Whiteheadian application of a Jamesian (1890) psychology within the field of quantum physics. This chapter considers the merit of a psychology as it pertains to nonhuman things. Since Harman's (2002/2006) Object-oriented Ontology proposes a similar project for the philosophical tradition of phenomenology, the similarly speculative proposal for psychology will be called Object-oriented Psychology (OOP).

The proposal for OOP will begin with a theoretical defense grounded upon Whiteheadian process as it has been supplied by Hartshorne (1977) and Griffin (1977). Both follow Whitehead's (1929/1978, 1933/1967) suggestion that the mind/body problem is really no problem at all since every entity is in part psychical and in part physical—varying only by degree. This avoids the problem of how a psychical entity can have an effect on a physical entity since it is understood from the outset that every actual entity includes both elements. Hartshorne describes this through his commitment to panpsychism. He argues that knowledge of human psychology—for example, the emotions of depression or excitement—can be insightfully applied to botany or geology. Griffin provides more of a logical proof for an OOP that follows from Whiteheadian process. The theoretical proposals for OOP are followed by the theoretical defense for an Object-oriented Ontology supplied by Harman (2002/2006; 2005). Following Heidegger's (1927/1962) analysis of equip-mentality, Harman makes a phenomenological argument for a non-anthropocentric world of objects. Harman's objects are understood through their many-sidedness—the side that is available to human sense-perception is merely one available side. Thus, a psychology of objects must do more to investigate the ontological breadth of objects. Between the arguments presented by Whitehead, Hartshorne, Griffin, and Harman, it is not evident that OOP provides anything beyond metaphysical speculation, which necessarily errs on the side of anthropomorphism (assuming, like Hartshorne, that objects must emote in a manner similar to humans). In any case, the discussion can only proceed from an anthropocentric agenda—being asked and studied *by* humans and *for* humans. Instead of arguing for the impossibility of any OOP project, this paper endeavors to provide the necessary and naïve first steps in the direction of what will likely emerge as a more sophisticated and insightful format for OOP.

## WHITEHEAD'S MANDATE FOR METAPHYSICS IN PSYCHOLOGY: APPLYING THE PRINCIPLES ELSEWHERE

A recent review of the literature demonstrates how well Alfred North Whitehead is known for his courage, wonder, creativity, and boldness (Shaviro, 2012; Stengers, 2012; Stenner, 2008; Harman 1997/2011). It comes as little surprise that his insights for the discipline of psychology would follow a similar trajectory of unthinkable boldness and novelty. Indeed, a psychology of objects or an OOP certainly tests the methodological temper of contemporary psychologists; doing so seems scarcely conceivable. Following the parameters of the early project of psychology, one finds that this typically unites the *experiencing subject* with the *object of experience* (Wundt, 1897, p. 3). The nexus of the psychological subject-matter is decidedly human. However, in order to demonstrate an OOP, it must be argued that an object does not need to be entertained by a human subject in order for the former to be psychological in nature. This is to say that in order for an object to be available to psychological experience, it need only be psychological in part. Griffin (1977) provides one such argument when he writes that "Whitehead holds that there is only one kind of actuality. All actual entities, even non-living ones, are 'organisms.' Inorganic, living, and conscious organisms are only different in degree, not in kind" (p. 133). In order for an object to contribute to experience as *an object of experience*, the object must itself be capable of psychological experience; objects of experience must be psychological in nature and not simply available to the psychological experience of a particular human subject. If psychology is useful in understanding the interaction between humans and objects, then by extension it must also be useful in understanding the interaction between objects and objects. This recognizes the constituents of psychics and physics in the undivided fabric of nature. Whitehead (1933/1967) explains:

> But any doctrine which refuses to place human experience outside nature, must find in descriptions of human experience factors which also enter into the descriptions of less specialized natural occurrences. If there be no such factors, then the doctrine of human experience as a fact within nature is mere bluff, founded upon vague phrases whose sole merit is a comforting familiarity. We should either admit dualism, at least as a provisional doctrine, or we should point out the identical elements connecting human experience with physical science. (185)

This de-anthropomorphization of objects is precisely the kind of daring that Whitehead (1929/1978) advocates in the practice of metaphysics. Griffin (1977) describes the responsibility of any metaphysician or scientist as Whitehead sees it:

> The method of metaphysics is to begin with factors based upon one topic of human interest, such as physics or psychology, imaginatively to generalize those factors in such a way that they might apply to all fields of interest, and then to test these generalizations by trying to apply them to the facts in these other fields. (p. 122)

According to Griffin, it is the responsibility of the discipline of psychology to imaginatively generalize the factors of psychology to associated fields of interest to see what works and what does not. It is fitting that OOP aims at an application of psychology, which seems counterintuitive—the psychology of

*Chapter 8*

things absent humans. It also follows from this that an unsuccessful proposal of OOP does not mean that no such application is possible. Instead, it means that a successful OOP has not yet reached a successful formulation.

Griffin suggests a possible starting point for an OOP for which Hartshorne may be found providing a few examples. The psychologist must first begin with that which is most familiar—namely, the psychology of human persons.

> If human experience is genuinely a part of nature, and if there be only one type of actual entity within nature ..., then, since it is that part of nature one knows most intimately, it provides the best starting point for finding principles that can be generalized to all actual entities. (Griffin, 1977, p. 124)

It could entirely be the case that the application of psychological principles to the study of plants demonstrates the lack of insight that psychology has for botany; but it could also be the case that psychology might open up a peculiar and unprecedented botanical world. Watson (1930) can be found doing the same thing in an attempt to develop the fledgling scientific discipline of psychology. He applies the principles of mechanical physics and physiology to human behavior with some exorbitantly optimistic expectations. Classical conditioning had been advertised as a replacement to parenting, teaching, training, and counseling. After several decades of tests and developments, its effectiveness had fallen short of its original expectations. But Watson exemplifies the courage, daring, and boldness for which Whitehead was well known. Moreover, it set the theoretical groundwork for the operant conditioning program of B.F. Skinner, which continues today.

## Roadblocks to Object-oriented Psychology

An obvious problem for a psychology of things is that of anthropomorphism. Psychology is a discipline that has been developed *by* humans and *for* humans. The emphasis of psychological science is human experience, a detail that has been labored over throughout the history of the discipline. Moreover, the theoretical defense of an OOP has been by way of generalizing human experience to the experience of things. This makes OOP anthropomorphic by nature. Watson's mechanomorphic conception of humans was used as an example of generalizing one field of inquiry (engineering) to another. This suggests that the anthropomorphism of objects might actually be called for when applying Whitehead's metaphysical edicts to psychology. Indeed, the goal might be understood as the insights to be gained by anthropomorphizing objects. Thus, an OOP may be proposed and tested, but this cannot be done without anthropomorphizing objects. This means that it fails the aspirations of the project of posthumanism, which aim at a conception of nature, which decenters the human (e.g., Wolfe, 2009).

Anthropomorphism is not the only problem that plagues the establishment of OOP. OOP must also necessarily be speculative in nature. This could well be applauded by a group of continental thinkers (Bryant et al., 2011) that have adopted the moniker "Speculative Realism," but it has been the bogeyman of psychology since James (1890/2007). Watson's mechanimorphization of humans (and animals) breaks down because there are tendencies in humans and animals that cannot be explained by a philosophy of mechanism. This has been established repeatedly in the middle of the twentieth century (Wertheimer 1938; Koch 1959; Köhler 1947/1957; Goldstein 1934/1995). Phenomenology (e.g., Husserl 1931/2002; Merleau-Pony 1945/1962) has been proposed as an alternative to a mechanized rendering of human experience, but this is only avoids the aforementioned pitfalls because humans are both sentient *and* sensible (Merleau-Ponty, 1964/1968). Thus, the errors of a mechanical model of experience can be explored phenomenologically *in humans*. OOP calls for an investigation that cannot be successfully carried out. Humans are capable of being measured objectively and subjectively. Objects may only be measured objectively; their subjective experience—which is already anthropomorphism—is inaccessible. Thus, OOP is necessarily speculative. Hartshorne (1977) demonstrates this point:

> We know what it is like to be a person studying rocks or molecules, in a sense in which we do not know what it is like to be a rock or a molecule. ... But, with a rock, all that we seem to have are our human perceptions of it, these perceptions being how the rock influences our psychophysical being under certain conditions. We know the rock 'from the outside,' ourselves 'from the inside.' We know animality by being an animal; we do not know inanimate nature by being inanimate. (90)

This is an important concession, but it does not necessarily mean that such a program is without merit. It could well be the case that it is time for a recrudescence of speculative metaphysics, and that psychology must adapt in order to be a valid twenty-first century discipline. Hartshorne speculates the possible merit of an OOP when he writes about how psychics may be explored in vegetation and geology:

> Just as physics generalizes variables of movement so that they can apply not only to a human hunter and his fleeing prey, but also to stars, planets, atoms, and photons, so psychics needs to generalize such ideas as feeling, perceiving, remembering, anticipating, intending, liking, and disliking, so that they can apply not only to animals, but even to the real individual constituents of the vegetable and mineral portions of nature. (90)

And continues, asking the questions that will lay the foundation for any researcher interested in OOP:

> Modern botany accepts the cell theory of living things. All living things that we can see without a microscope consist of many far smaller living things that we cannot see, each of which is an organized individual. Is there a psychology of single cells? They do react to stimuli, and they do organize their internal activities remarkably well. This is most obvious in single-celled animals and plants, but I believe it is a reasonable assumption in all cells. It follows that, even if it is right (and some dispute this) to deny feeling or sensation to a tree or flowering plant, still the cells of which trees or plants consist may feel, may enjoy their activities. In that case, mind in some form may pervade the entire kingdom of living things. I take this view... (91)

The latter half of this quote demonstrates Hartshorne's panpsychism. This follows from the argument that lines cannot be drawn to separate nature into mutually exclusive orders—e.g., living nature cannot be separated from non-living nature because parts of the living are lifeless and the reverse. Hartshorne applies the same reasoning to the parts of human anatomy. If it hurts when one feels sad, then by extension one could maintain that one's finger is sad after closing it in a car-door.

> Take the case of pain. We have this feeling if certain cells of ours undergo damage. But if the cells have their own feelings, they can hardly enjoy being damaged. So what is our suffering but our participating in their suffering? Hurt certain of my cells and you hurt me. Hurt my friend and you hurt me. My cells are the friends I have always with me and always care about, whereas my other friends I may be separated from and may forget or learn to dislike. The mind-body relation, I suggest, as Plato hinted long ago, is a relation of sympathy; it is the most instinctive of all forms of sympathy, the form we are born with and do not have to learn. I seriously believe, and not alone I, that this is the key to the influence of body upon mind. There is mind on both sides of the relation, but mind on very different levels. The gap between the levels is crossed by a kind of sympathy. We share in the emotional life of our cells. That is why, in good health, we can have a feeling of wellbeing. (92-93)

Once again, Hartshorne's panpsychism follows from Whitehead's metaphysical edicts for a creative and courageous application of psychology outside of its traditional parameters. However, given the necessarily speculative nature of this theory, it would be difficult to judge the usefulness of Hartshorne's panpsychism as a method in OOP. In his specific example, an experimental group might be constructed where chronic pain sufferers trained to empathize with the tissue implicated in their pain. This application falls outside of the scope of phenomenological psychophysics because the organic tissue in question is not capable of reporting its subjective experience. Indeed, its subjective experience exists only by-way-of the experimental investigator.

Roadblocked or not, what follows is an argument for a psychological world of objects *sans* humans. The history of the discipline of psychology from Wundt onward has maintained the psychological import of objects *insofar as they contribute to experience*. Thus, psychological objects are objects-for-human-subjects. This does not mean that objects only exist for human subjects, but that the psychological import of objects may only be understood from the vantage point of human subjects. Object-oriented Psychology must defend a psychology of objects without humans. To begin, this paper will follow the argument of Harman that objects have a life of ontological complexity and depth all by themselves. Harman (2002/2006) uses Heidegger's (1927/1962) analysis of equipmentality to defend the many-sidedness of objects and their dynamic capacity to entertain other objects.

## OBJECTS WITHOUT HUMANS

Momentarily suspended is the assumption that objects gain existential and ontological depth only when magically intended by subjects. Harman (2002/2006) explains that this is to suppose "that only human beings transcend, as if the objects surrounding us were only dreary present-at-hand lumps that needed a 'human touch' to come to life" (p. 92). Here Harman introduces the language of Heidegger's (1927/1962) analysis of equipment. While this will be examined at length below, for now it is sufficient to note that "present-at-hand" refers to the objects caricatured as those that lie dormant, awaiting the touch of a human. For Heidegger, this life-giving subject is Dasein, and the otherwise dead objects may be understood as those presupposed by the constancy hypothesis of modernists and rejected by Kantian correlationism. Heidegger compares "present-at-hand lumps" with the "ready-to-hand" objects of human intentionality; the latter instance is where they are understood to come to life. As such, objects are only meaningful insofar as a human is using them—a notion that Harman is challenging. He continues,

> It might even be the case that, like the menacing toys prowling in some depraved Gepetto's workship, objects truly flourish only in the midnight reality that shields them from our view. Perhaps entities are actually rendered bland or unidimensional only *through* their contact with humans. Perhaps instead of *liberating* objects into a clearing, Dasein is actually guilty of *chloroforming* the things, of pinning them down like the exterminated moths that bulk up an amateur's private collection. (p. 92)

Like Merleau-Ponty (1964/1968), who challenges the notion that a single consciousness orchestrates all of his limbs by proposing an equally probably alternative scenario, Harman proposes an alternative to the subject-object relationship that normally privileges the subject. If there is no way to compare my experience of the cashmere sweater when it's not being worn for a romantic date, how can I justify that it is the latter event that best demonstrates the ontological depth of the sweater? Suspending this assumption gives rise to a novel consideration of the being of objects.

Before getting into Heidegger's analysis of objects as equipment or tools, consider Whitehead's (1933/1967) guidelines for the examination of subject-object occasions. Instead of beginning with the subject who brings objects into being, Whitehead indicates the reality that must immediately precede a particular subjective experience:

> The process of experiencing is constituted by the reception of entities, whose being is antecedent to that process, into the complex fact which is that process itself. These antecedent entities, thus received as factors into the process of experiencing, are termed 'objects' for that experiential occasion. Thus primarily the term 'object' expresses the relation of the entity, thus denoted, to one or more occasions of experiencing. Two conditions must be fulfilled in order that an entity may function as an object in a process of experience: (1) the entity must be *antecedent,* and (2) the entity must be experienced in virtue of its antecedence; it must be *given.* Thus an object must be a thing received, and must not be either a mode of reception or a thing *generated* in that occasion. Thus the process of experiencing is constituted by the reception of objects into the unity of that complex occasion which is the process itself. The process creates itself, but it does not create the objects which it receives as factors in its own nature. (pp. 178-179)

There is much to be taken from Whitehead's outline of investigation. He repeats that the object that is entertained by an experiencing subject must be antecedent to the event of its entertainment. Thus the term "object" denotes the *relational capacity* toward a subject and not the other way around. In case this is unclear, he again stresses that "an object must be a thing received, and must not be either a mode of reception or a thing *generated* in that occasion." Indeed, Whitehead seems to be indicating an object-in-itself. This object is marked by certain characteristics through which it may be entertained by subjects and into subject-object events. Furthermore, the subject-object event must *not* exhaust the potentiality of the object, for the object is *antecedent* to its mode of reception.

Following Whitehead's guidelines, what remains is an analysis of the object-object relationship. Like the analysis of the experiencing subject, it will be demonstrated that objects also occupy the world in certain discrete ways as well as through an unapproachably infinite limit of possible ways. The finitude and infinitude that characterize objects can also be found folding in upon one another in a reversibility that suggests that 'mere' objects are just as profound and nuanced as the philosophers who entertain them in late-hour ruminations.

In order to engage the relational capacity of objects, Heidegger's (1927/1962) impressive analysis of equipmentality will be taken up. As indicated in its brief presentation above, Heidegger seems to defend a human-centric reality. However, if the same analysis is read through a Whiteheadian lens (e.g., Harman 1997/2010), the human privilege dissipates. "If we read Heidegger's tool-analysis in the right way, the lingering priority of Dasein in his philosophy is vaporized, and we encounter a strange new world filled with schooling possibilities for twenty-first century philosophy" (2002/2006, p. 2). Harman argues that the dual-relationality between human subjects and the objects they entertain applies equally well to objects' relationships with other objects. This reversibility of Heidegger's equipmental analysis of objects begins to resemble the reversibility of *flesh* discussed in the previous section. That is, just as a human subject can be present to themselves as an object, so too can objects occupy radically different forms of being. Harman explains:

> The analysis of equipment is *not* a limited regional description of hammers, saws, toothpicks, and other technical devices. Rather, the famous tool-analysis holds good for *all* entities, no matter how useful or useless they might be. *Beings themselves* are caught up in a continual exchange between presence-at-hand and readiness-to-hand. (p. 4)

Harman summarizes the risk of mining Heidegger's analysis of equipment for its most radical conclusions:

> We are finally in a position to oppose the long dictatorship of human beings in philosophy. What emerges in its place is a ghostly cosmos in which humans, dogs, oak trees, and tobacco are on precisely the same footing as glass bottles, pitchforks, windmills, comets, ice cubes, magnets, and atoms. (p. 2)

This, it should be noted, is precisely what happened when Whitehead had been applied to the experiencing subject.

## HEIDEGGER'S ANALYSIS OF EQUIPMENT: TOOL-BEING AND ITS REVERSAL

Recall Heidegger's contribution the earlier review of nature's bifurcation. His (1927/1962) investigation of Being identified a modernist preoccupation with ontic forms of being. This is the kind of being understood as a matter of fact. Taken up in the practice of science, Heidegger has noted how this leads to the production of manuals for the sake of more manuals. This was contrasted with the ontological form of becoming. This is understood as the mode of Being that is always in the process of creation and discovery. Given the dynamic form of nature allowed by Heidegger's ontological hermeneutic, scientific practice continues through novel production, transformation, and becoming. Here one finds no end-goal to scientific practice; the book never closes on nature's investigation. It is evident from his analysis of Modern philosophy that a preoccupation with ontic being couldn't be more tiresome. We can follow a similar differentiation with respect to objects in Heidegger's analysis of equipment. Here one finds that objects also manifest with a two-fold purpose.

Borrowing from the ontic-ontological distinction, we can understand objects in two different ways. Harman (2002/2006) explains how "there are two separate facets to equipment: (1) its irreducibly veiled activity, and (2) its sensible and explorable profile. In more familiar Heideggerian terms, there is the tool viewed "ontologically" and the same tool viewed "ontically" (p. 22). As an ontic thing, objects have particular qualities and characteristics that can presumably be known in advance. These are objective characteristics that cannot in principle participate in events, because we have already learned that events are dynamic. This leaves the ontological thing: the characteristic of an ontological thing is that it can only participate in events. No quality can be said about an ontological thing because this quality could not in principle participate in an event. We thus find two mutually exclusive modes of the being of objects. In the first instance objects can be described in great detail, but these objects may never take part in subject-object events. In the second instance we find objects that cannot be described, but are able to participate in all manner of events. This is how we may begin to distinguish between objects that are present-at-hand from those ready-to-hand. Heidegger (1927/1962) explains,

> The kind of Being which equipment possesses—in which it manifests itself in its own right—we call "*readiness-to-hand.*" Only because equipment has *this* 'Being-in-itself' and does not merely occur, is it manipulable in the broadest sense and at our disposal. No matter how sharply we just *look* at the 'outward appearance' of Things in whatever form this takes, we cannot discover anything read-to-hand. (p. 98)

Here he provides the full description of objects that have the character of ready-to-hand: "it is manipulable in the broadest sense and at our disposal"— that is, it is available to be taken up in a host of projects for which it is uniquely suited and subject to its absorption therein. Heidegger also indicates the ineffability of objects that have the character of ready-to-hand: "No matter how sharply we just *look* at the 'outward appearance' ... we cannot discover anything ready-to-hand." Heidegger provides the description of objects that have the character of present-at-hand by negation of those ready-to-hand: "The ready-to-hand becomes deprived of its worldhood so that Being-just-present-at-hand comes to the fore" (106). Just in case there was any confusion as to Heidegger's opinion regarding objects that have the character of presence-at-hand, he has included the indicated their measly stature by prefixing it with the adjective "just." Harman (2002/2006) provides the following commentary:

> The goal of Martin Heidegger's career was to identify and to attack the notion of reality as something present-at-hand. ... Heidegger's error lies in the assumption, typical of the post-Kantian era, that a reflection on *human being* is the key to passing from an unphilosophical perspective to a philosophical one. Heidegger seems to think that human *use* of objects is what gives them ontological depth, frees them from their servitude as mere slabs of present-at-hand physical matter. And this is the point at which contemporary philosophy needs to part company with Heidegger in the most radical way: *objects themselves are already more than present-at-hand*. The interplay of dust and cinder blocks and shafts of sunlight is haunted by the drama of presence and withdrawal no less than are language or lurid human moods. As a result, philosophy must break loose from the textual and linguistic ghetto that it has been constructing for itself, and return to the drama of the things themselves. (p. 16)

At any moment, an object may express the character of readiness-to-hand or "just" presence-at-hand. In the former, the object is absorbed into the project of a subject as part an event. In the latter, the object stands opposed to the project of a subject as if announcing its obstinacy in specific ways. One sees how an object that is absorbed into a subject-object event could never be identified with particular characteristics. Similarly evident in the latter case is the manner by which objects refuse to participate in a particular event. Here they effectively announce those very qualities through which they refuse participation! Heidegger maintains that the everyday experience of subjects (human and otherwise) takes up objects as equipment in these two ways. But this neat demarcation between ready-to-hand and present-at-hand does not satisfy the variety of subject-object relations. While the totality of objects prehended in a multiplicity of ways might certainly be separated into instances of readiness-to-hand and presence-at-hand, this does not mean that any one object can ever be placed into either category. Indeed, the reversibility discussed earlier applies even to the being of objects. Following Harman (2002/2006), this will be referred to as tool-being.

Consider a scene from the baseball-diamond, chosen in honor of OOO's progenitor: a pitcher has just forced an infield fly-ball for the final out of the ballgame. This scene will be analyzed carefully in order to demonstrate the variety of ways that tool-being might manifest. For example, the pitcher's infielders comprise the equipmental totality that supports the likely conclusion that the last pitch of the game has been thrown. Even though the shortstop and second basemen are persons of infinite ontological depth—each with their own uniquely nuanced pre-game rituals—to the pitcher, they are run-preventing defensive-tools that keep fly-balls from hitting the infield dirt. That is, we find that the relationship between two persons—pitcher and

shortstop—fits the subject-tool mold. The other scenario provides the same
subject-tool mold but does so without presupposing that tool-being is limited
to particular types of entities. In it one finds no persons at all—only objects.
It is in these scenarios that we find the domestic world of Heidegger's tool-
shop expanding outward to the public world:

> Any work with which one concerns oneself is ready-to-hand not only in the
> domestic world of the workshop but also in the *public world*. Along with the
> public world, the *environing Nature* is discovered and is accessible to every-
> one. In roads, streets, bridges, buildings, our concern discovers Nature as
> having some definite direction. (p. 100)

Each object is an instance of tool-being, capable of being swept up and
utilized in a particular way by a subject but always occupying definite space
and providing particular capacities. Consider the above pitcher who believes
that he has just delivered the last pitch of the ball game. The ball did not fly
over the backstop, nor did it find a gap between the extended lateral movement of the first and second basemen. Retrieving this baseball is well within
the capacity of the pitcher's defense-tool. The several million blades of outfield grass that run from second base to the warning track are absorbed into
the small halo around the shortstop who is prepared to make the catch. While
the center-fielder's vertical leap, the first-baseman's hand-eye coordination,
and the catcher's quick reflexes are all potentialities of the pitcher's defense-
tool, each is irrelevant to the event that is currently unfolding. Indeed, each of
these capacities, along with the shortstop's ability to catch a fly-ball, are
absorbed into the entire ready-to-hand equipmental totality of the visiting
team's defensive infield. Until, of course, the second-basemen collides with
the shortstop and the ball bounces into the outfield grass. The pitcher's
defense-tool has broken down. The formerly camouflaged occupants of the
equipmental totality of visiting-team's defense-tool announce the singular-
ities of their being as they pertain to the now unfolding event-structure.
Though superfluous moments before, the third-basement is suddenly found
occupying a space with a definite proximity to the embarrassing jumble of
infielders, and the left-fielder's top-end leg speed becomes integral to the
pitcher's recalibrated defensive-tool.

## Tool, Broken-tool, and Their Reversibility

We learn a few interesting details from this equipmental breakdown. Initially, the ontological identity of the visiting team as defensive tool is wrapped
up in the successful retrieval of the infield fly-ball. We find that part of the
living identity of objects as ready-to-hand tools is in partial concealment.
This has been well-documented by Heidegger and the scholars of his work.
But we also see various other object-relations that are occurring within and

about the particular instance of defensive tool-being—additional events that do not necessarily engage our protagonist pitcher. These two details will be discussed in turn.

While some elements are integral to this task—for example, the shortstop's proximity to and view of the descending baseball—others are superfluous: that the center-fielder led the league in stolen home-runs is of little consequence to the event that occupies him at present. Thus, even though we see a specific capacity of tool-being while at work in a particular event, no event can in principle exhaust the ontological capacity of tool-being: elements of tool-being always remain partially veiled while at work. This is true even of the shortstop, upon whom the eyes of thirty-thousand spectators descend—indeed, his capacity to rifle the ball to the first baseman's chest is not currently on display. Nor, for that matter, is his capacity to make his daughter giggle with delight. When drawn into an event, an object demonstrates a limited number of available capacities—that is, even when brought to life, an object is still only partially lit-up. Harman (2002/2006) writes,

> It is the nature of tool-being to recede from every view. In the strict sense, we can never know just *what* equipment is. Like the giant squids of the Marianas Trench, tool-beings are encountered only once they have washed up dead on shore, no longer immersed in their withdrawn reality. (pp. 4-5)

Moreover, since we have learned from Heidegger that each instance of an object's readiness-to-hand results in its transformation, an object can never be investigated in its entirety. Here one runs into the limit of Heidegger's animated beings.

In the event of the infield fly-ball, one also finds definite material capacities and limitations within its present-at-hand tool-being. The shortstop cannot, for instance, soar into the air to meet the baseball at the apex of its flight. We also see from the second-baseman's interference that these otherwise veiled capacities of defensive tool-being are continued despite their presence-at-hand. With the baseball suspended in mid-air, a survey of the field would still find the dirt compressing beneath the catcher's cleats, strings of leather holding together the third-baseman's worn-out glove, and the backstop net vigilantly protecting spectators from errant balls. From Heidegger's analysis of tools put to work by human use, these capacities disappear into a single unified tool-being. Despite the spectral limitations it imposes on spectators, the backstop netting is accommodated by vision and disappears into the baseball scene. It remains absent from the world until disrupted by a line-drive foul-ball at which point its materiality becomes appreciably apparent. When put to use by humans, objects occupy this space of capacity-amplification and reduction. Yet neither in amplification nor in reduction does an object's tool-being exhaust its being. However, instead of arguing that this continued retreat of tool-being into the shadows makes their investigation unmanageable, Harman (2002/2006) explains that this *rejuvenates* the world of objects:

> That tool-beings retreat into a silent background means not only that they are invisible to humans, but that they exceed any of their interactions with other tool-beings. In this sense, tool-beings are unearthly, otherworldly. Then far from *abolishing* the transcendent world of things in themselves, Heidegger inadvertently *rejuvenates* this notion in a form that no dialectic can overcome. In this respect, he is a full step beyond most of his successors, who continue to wage war against a naïve brand of Billiard Ball Realism that is no longer a threat to anyone. (p. 5)

The backstop net does not hang idly by until called into action by the several hundred intending humans who perilously face a careening foul-ball. This is a reproduction of the modernist assumption of objects that supposes that they simply remain where they were left, and do so inactively. Whitehead (1933/1967) explains how "[t]hus viewed in abstraction objects are passive, but viewed in conjunction they carry the creativity which drives the world. The process of creation is the form of unity of the Universe" (p. 179). In the passive form, we understand the ontic identity of beings. Take the backstop net as an example: it was created by humans for human protection from foul balls. It will hang there until it no longer protects humans from foul balls, at which point a human will take it down and replace it or update it. This backstop net could also be viewed creatively, as though it were always participating in the events of Nature. Objects may be thus classified:

> The initial situation with its creativity can be termed the initial phase of the new occasion. It can equally well be termed the 'actual world' relative to that occasion. ... It can thus be termed a 'real potentiality.' The 'potentiality' refers to a passive capacity, the term 'real' refers to the creative activity.... (p. 179)

At each moment, objects may be classified as a 'real potentiality.' For the shortstop, the real includes all of the processes and capacities that are engaged in the successful retrieval of the fly-ball; the potential includes the sum total of available capacities that remain veiled. As soon as the baseball hits the dirt, the shortstop's ability to rifle the ball to the first-baseman's chest becomes real, and the fly-ball retrieval becomes a potentiality (or a null potentiality). The tool-being of the short-stop, wielded by the pitcher, is a real potentiality—the sum of unearthed capacities and current engagements. By smooshing them together, Whitehead indicates the interconnection of these modes of tool-being. We understand that these modes of tool-being fold over upon one another to such a degree that readiness-to-hand is always on the verge of becoming mere presence-at-hand, and vice-versa. While this distinction is easily introduced into the tool-being of a shortstop, consider also the backstop net, the plot of real-estate upon which the stadium was built, or the chemical reactions taking place in the megawatt fluorescent stadium light-bulbs. Harman (2002/2006) explains,

> It is crucial to note that this is not restricted to tools of human origin: there are also dependable earth-formations that provide useful caravan routes or hold back the sea. At each moment, the world is a geography of objects, whether these objects are made of the latest plastics or were born at the dawn of time (p. 21)

Each of these objects may be understood in terms of the multiplicity of lives that are found within their capacity—lives that do not require the human to initiate. Considering objects from the perspective of humans is simply one way of doing so. Since the present project is interested in decentering the human, this perspective will be presently suspended. This allows for a more expanded conception of the object-relations within Nature. Whitehead (1933/1967) also notes that the human perspective is just *one* special life-thread of a unified Nature:

> This is at once the doctrine of the unity of nature, and of the unity of each human life. The conclusion follows that our consciousness of the self-identity pervading our life-thread of occasions, is nothing other than knowledge of a special strand of unity within the general unity of nature. It is a locus within the whole, marked out by its own peculiarities, but otherwise exhibiting the general principle which guides the constitution of the whole. This general principle is the object-to-subject structure of experience. (Whitehead, pp. 187-188)

Continuing, the object-to-subject relationship will be considered absent the assumption that their only meaningful interaction takes place via an intentional human.

## THE OBJECT IN-ITSELF

The argument that objects have a life outside of human interaction is a realist claim. This is precisely what is being developed here. This one is not the orthodox nineteenth-century brand of realism, but one that is defended by phenomenology. This is an unusual point of departure given phenomenology's penchant for criticizing all forms of realism. As Harman (2002/2006, 2011) and Meillassoux (2006/2012) have observed, phenomenology and other continental schools of thought have developed principally in their opposition to realism. However, a phenomenological defense of realism isn't as oxymoronic as it might at first appear.

Consider three instances of ontological arguments *against* realism that support a new, more sophisticated brands of realism. The first, of course, is Whitehead's (1933/1967) above claim that objects are antecedent to events—this follows his systematic critique of Modern Science (1925/1953) for its regular commission of the fallacy of misplaced concreteness; second is the first-personal epistemology of Michael Polanyi (1958), which is used to defend a gestalt-perception based realism (1964); third is Husserl's (1931/2002) dismissal of the constancy-hypothesis brand of realism in order to promote a well known transcendental science focused on things themselves. To this list I would like to add Heidegger's (1927/1962) analysis of equipment and Merleau-Ponty's (1942/1962) perception of objects.

## Heidegger's Objects

From his aforementioned critique of modernist philosophy and science, we find that Heidegger deplores the endless cataloging of the ontic characteristics of things. These are things by themselves, sucked into a vacuum and incapable of interacting with other beings or things. These are objects present-at-hand. Instead of this being *the* mode of being of objects, it has been noted that this is *a* mode of being—that is, ontic being. While such descriptions of objects can be extensive and reliable, these descriptions never enter into relationships with other beings and things. When objects are swept up into relationship, they come to life and enter into the process of transformation characteristic of ontological being. Objects demonstrate ontic modes of being as well as ontological modes of being, and these two modes fold over upon one another in what we have called the reversibility of objects (following the language of Merleau-Ponty from chapter six). This seems to promote a realism wherein objects exist in-themselves only when they have the ontic character of being—that is to say, objects are only objects when they're not doing anything. We have already discussed the mutual exclusivity of ontic and ontological modes of being, but now we must demonstrate that this is not of the *either/or* variety. That is, objects are not *either* ontic *or* ontological, but always both—just as subjects and objects may always be separated into the same categories. It is here that one finds Heidegger's sophisticated brand of realism.

Objects can always be understood as an endless list of characteristics—for example, the trading card of the shortstop from before lists his ontic capacity for offensive-tool-being and defensive-tool-being. Moreover, you or I might run into said shortstop *as* a .287 batting average, thirty-eight home-runs, or a blown nineth-inning third-out. While being thus engaged, the offensive- or defensive-tool-being might present a here-to-for unseen side of him or itself that demands an expansion of ontic-tool-being. Does one face the ontological shortstop or the ontic shortstop? At which point does the tool break down? Does the tool ever break down? Can it break down without its user noticing? Can a tool ever break down and leave its user in ontological suspension? Instead of conceiving the reversibility of being as a mutually exclusive relationship where the two are continually tagging in and out, we find that they are always engaged though in different ways, and never exhausted.

While the example of the human aptly demonstrates the reversibility of being, the goal here is not to defend Heidegger as a correlationist, but as a realist—one who does only consider humans in-themselves, but considers objects in-themselves as well. From the earlier discussion of equipmentality, Heidegger (1927/1962) points to the world of tool-being outside of the workshop—he calls this the *"public world"* (p. 100). He continues, "A covered railway platform takes account of bad weather; an installation for public lighting takes account of the darkness, or rather of specific changes in the presence or absence of daylight—the 'position of the sun'" (p. 101). For a moment, Heidegger's ontological character as a humanist-tool breaks down, and gives up the richness and depth of the world of objects—objects without any humans to engage them. While he might certainly be discarded along with broken bicycle chains, are we to understand that a broken tool is a reduction to mere presence-at-hand? By no means! Perhaps his capacity for tool-being requires expansion to allow for additional possibilities—the additional possibilities that he has generously extended to covered railway platforms and public lighting installations. These, it seems, have an ontological depth more akin to Dasein than to billiard balls. This is why Harman explains that "Heidegger's account of equipment gives birth to an ontology of *objects themselves.* Contrary to the usual view, tool-being does not describe objects insofar as they are handy implements employed for human purposes" (2002/2006, p. 1). Indeed, Heidegger is not being painted as a "billiard ball realist," but as a realist in the sense of Whitehead's objects which have "real potentiality."

## Merleau-Ponty's Objects

Perhaps the most formidable argument against the realism that is here proposed comes from Merleau-Ponty's *Phenomenology of Perception*. Recall earlier how Merleau-Ponty (1964/1968) himself has accused *Phenomenology of Perception* of being too lopsided in its consideration of consciousness as the mediation of all things. However, like Heidegger immediately above, even Merleau-Ponty's Humanist-tool-being breaks down in an unexpected flight toward that which would characterize his later work.

Like Polanyi and Husserl, Merleau-Ponty (1942/1962) has followed the Gestalt theory's dismissal of the constancy hypothesis but, instead of looking to the object-form, he begins with consciousness. Perception is the point of departure, for it is here that everything begins. In order to understand that world, one must begin with perception.

In one instance, he suggests the untenability of positing an object in-itself. For Merleau-Ponty, all prehended objects are prehended *from a particular vantage point.* In the preceding discussion, this is why an object is always partially veiled. Even the shortstop, with the thirty-thousand sets of eyes descending upon him, is partially veiled—not only is this still a limited number of spectral angles, but it is also a limited number of contexts and occasions. To talk of a cup or table that exists in-itself, is to suggest that everything it has possibly done or can do has been cross-examined. Merleau-Ponty suggests that a perceived object never makes it this far. Indeed, to consider an object in terms of its availability to 360-degrees of visible access is to suggest that it could unfold in the presence of an observer in order to reveal each of its sides at once, and no such perspective exists.

> For example, I see the next-door house from a certain angle, but it would be seen differently from the right bank of the Seine, or from the inside, or again from an aeroplane: the house *itself* is none of these appearances; it is, as Leibniz said, the flat projection of these perspectives and of all possible perspectives, that is, the perspectiveless position from which all can be derived, the house seen from nowhere. (p. 67)

Merleau-Ponty seems to suggest that the house seen from all possible perspectives would be some sort of geometrical ideal—the house as navigated with the aid of digital software with which it can be rotated on a computer screen. Indeed, this is the house devoid of any ontological being: the house as the aggregation of ontic spectral characteristics. This, it seems, is no house at all—at least not as perceived by a human. It certainly isn't a house that can begin to collect dust, tenants, and memories. Here Merleau-Ponty provides a cogent argument *against* realism: an object cannot have any meaningful or impactful existence in-itself; it is always limited to an existence *for* an observer. Absent the human, an object is limited to an ontic catalog, like a humanistic rendering of Heidegger's equipment. However, just like Heidegger, who carries his analysis of equipment into the private ruminations of railway platform-covers, Merleau-Ponty continues to inch toward the invisible objects in-themselves. He considers his meditation on the visual perception of objects,

> To see is to enter a universe of beings which *display themselves*, and they would not do this if they could not be hidden behind each other or behind me. In other words: to look at an object is to inhabit it, and from this habituation to grasp all things in terms of the aspect which they present to it. But in so far as I see those things too, they remain abodes open to my gaze, and, being potentially lodged in them, I already perceive from various angles the central object of

my present vision. Thus every object is the mirror of all others. When I look at the lamp on my table, I attribute to it not only the qualities visible from where I am, but also those which the chimney, the walls, the table can 'see'; the back of my lamp is nothing but the face which it 'shows to the chimney.' I can therefore see an object in so far as objects form a system or a world, and in so far as each one treats the others round it as spectators of its hidden aspects which guarantee the permanence of those aspects by their presence. Any seeing of an object by me is instantaneously repeated between all those objects in the world which are apprehended as co-existent, because each of them is all that the others 'see' of it. Our previous formula must therefore be modified: the house itself is not the house seen from nowhere, but the house seen from everywhere. The completed object is translucent, being shot through from all sides by an infinite number of present scrutinizes which intersect in its depths leaving nothing hidden. (pp. 68-69)

It becomes exceedingly difficult to maintain Merleau-Ponty's humanistic agenda in light of certain realist excursions into the geography of objects like this one here. He begins by slowly expanding the object as it appears to the human observer. The interplay between observer and observed is suggestive of the subject/object reversibility that he would propose later, but he still finds the central locus in the perceiving gaze. He then claims that "every object is the mirror of all others." This marks a point of departure. He does not suggest that an object is a mirror of the perceiver, but of all other objects. Anthropomorphisms aside, Merleau-Ponty extends his relationship with the lamp in order to consider the lamp's relations to other available objects. It could nearly be argued that Merleau-Ponty imagines the lamp as seen from the chimney as though the chimney provides just another vantage point that could be taken up. However, his additional observations make this argument unlikely. He claims that an object seen "is instantaneously repeated between all those objects in the world" and, furthermore, "each of them is all that the others 'see' of it." Thus, one finds that the being of an object in a particular moment is not limited to its engagement with a particular observer. Were two additional observers present, the one lamp must be taken across each of these intentionalities, and not as three separately intended lamps. If prehension is used to replace intentional consciousness, the lamp in-itself must include the prehending-prehended interrelationships of all present objects. Only here does one begin to understand the "real" lamp. But the "real" being—referring to the "real potentiality" of objects introduced by Whitehead, above—also does not exhaust the being of the lamp. To this one must also add the as yet untapped potentialities of being—those that presently lay dormant.

With Merleau-Ponty, one actually begins to understand the world of objects as they exist in-themselves. While the analysis of objects provided in *Phenomenology of Perception* takes up the being of objects from the vantage point of embodied consciousness, it is understood even here that the imperial human gaze presents one of many subjectivities by which objects might be entertained. This becomes particularly clear in *The Visible and the Invisible*. For Merleau-Ponty, the object in-itself must include the object as "seen" by every present object. This, of course, does not mean that an object is limited to spectral qualities. Just as sense-awareness is not limited to vision in humans, so too might it be understood that the visibility of an object is a euphemism for all availabilities of the latter to prehension.

Heidegger also selects the human as the point of departure into the being of objects, but this does not limit the being of things to their availability and unavailability to Dasein. The human simply provides an easily accessible example of how objects are readily absorbed into particular tasks. From the scenarios that introduced the section, the equipmental world of the pitcher has received the most attention. Here it was shown how baseball infielders can be taken up as equipmental objects of defensive tool-being. That is, beings with the undeniable capacity for the mode of being characteristic of Dasein can also be engaged with as tools when taken up as such. This happens whenever shortstops are glorified by trading cards or honored with Golden Glove Awards. In the spirit of the present object, we will now turn to beings with the undeniable capacity for the mode of being that is not characteristic of Dasein and consider them in the expanded ontological depth of tool-being.

## The Being of Objects, or Tool-being

It has been demonstrated that objects occupy a two-fold status in Nature. This object-duality may be understood as an ontic versus ontological, present-at-hand versus ready-to-hand, or potentiality versus real. Following Heidegger's lead, Harman suggests the term tool-being to refer to these dual identities. Similar to the way that Whitehead's term prehension expanded the subject-object relationship to allow for their reversibility, so too does Harman's tool-being allow for the reversibility between these object-dualities. In the previous section the concern was the subject-object relationship; of present concern is the object-subject relationship. The language of Whitehead will be used alongside that of Heidegger in the consideration of the second scenario that introduced this section.

## Tool-being of Bicycle Crank-arms

The pedals of a bicycle do not propel the latter forward. That is, the point of initiative contact between human and bicycle is not what directly causes the movement of the entire system. A bicycle-system's movement is contingent on a host of constitutive processes. Indeed, the rotation of pedals initiates a process of object-interrelations that, if connected in a particular way, results in the bicycle's forward movement. However, any breakdown between pedal rotation and bicycle-frame demonstrates the limited causal relationship between these two. Take, for simplicity's sake, the operations of the low-tech track-bicycle—the oldest technology in the world of cycling. Here one finds a bicycle frame with two wheels, a saddle, handlebars, and pedals—the eidetic structure of the bicycle as intended by a human. Seated upon the saddle with hands on the handlebars, pedal rotation results in the movement of the system. The self-consciousness of humans, wont to attribute volition and will to its engagements (as discussed in the previous section), acknowledges that the human is in control of the bicycle. This is not the case. Humans control processes several times removed from the final bicycle-moving cause. The focus at present will be on the bicycle's drivetrain—of which the pedals play an ancillary role. To avoid attributions to the managerial role played by humans, the bicycle will be considered after dismount—the balanced bicycle that rolls down a slight decline. Without the interference of a human, the bicycle pedals slowly rotate as the bicycle moves forward.

The pedals have internal bearings that allow for free-spinning and are each screwed into 170mm steel crank-arms. These steel arms are connected to one another and through the base of the bicycle frame via a bottom bracket, onto which they have been forced by several hundred pounds of pressure. This bottom bracket allows the crank-arm-system to rotate freely about the bicycle frame. It should be noted here that the bicycle pedals are typically viewed as two components of a bicycle's movement—its rider pushes the right, then left, then right, etc. These are actually two points of impact on a single system—like the left and right hands at ten-and-two of the automobile steering wheel. Moving on, there is a steel chain-ring that is bolted to the right crank arm so that it rotates along with the crank-arm-system. The outer edge of the chain-ring is covered in equally spaced out steel teeth. Into these teeth fit the links of a chain—each link comprising two plates and a bearing. The bearings of the links fit in between the teeth of the chain-ring so that the entire linked-chain-system is pulled along in the direction of the crank-arm-system. The chain is a single closed system that is pulled about an additional, smaller chain-ring. This chain-ring is locked onto the hub of a bicycle wheel that rotates about the lower-rear of the bicycle frame. The wheel is bolted to the frame, and its rotation is allowed by an internal bearing of the rear hub. If this rear hub chain-ring rotates, so does the wheel. Connected by the linked-chain, the rotation of the crank-arm-system co-occurs with the rotation of the rear hub/rear-wheel-system. Avoided here is the use of "cause" because the order could easily be reversed—spin the rear-wheel-system and the crank-arm-system also spins.

Here one finds the absorption of separate tool-beings into one drive-train-system. There are still plenty of processes to be considered before one begins to understand bicycle-movement, but this limited survey should suffice for the present discussion.

Again, efforts have been specifically taken to avoid the managerial role of the intentional human in the operation of this system. If it pleases the reader, imagine that the track-bicycle in question has just fallen out of a sporting-goods display case after being upset by a (naturally occurring) earthquake. Miraculously, it has managed to roll thirty-five feet before crashing into a shelving-unit holding a variety of fashionable yet modest tennis dresses. If witnessed, one would see the pedals rotating as if engaged by a ghost-rider. The attribution of the intentional human is difficult to avoid, even when it requires that said human have no corporeal body. Try to instead consider the tool-being of the crank-arm: the crank-arm prehends the chain-ring, bottom bracket, bicycle-frame, chain, and rear hub in very specific ways, drawing out of them a very particular form of tool-being. To say that the crank-arm supplies the will that gets the system in motion is just as reasonable as the attribution of a ghost-rider. Yet it still manages to co-participate in the drive-train-event. This particular ontological mode of crank-arm tool-being can be abruptly halted if any of the constituent event-objects were to break down. Consider, for instance, a single chain-link-plate that has been bent by an errant pebble. When this link is drawn into a tooth of the chain-ring, the bent plate separates from the adjoining link. No longer connected, these two adjacent ends of the chain continue around the chain-ring until gravity pulls one side of the chain downwards and away from the drive-train-system. One of two things can happen with respect to the crank-arm tool-being. If the chain falls between the chain-ring and the frame, then the crank-arm-system will become jammed and seize up—the crank-arm will come to a stop and the bicycle will come to a halt; if the chain falls outside of the chain-ring, then the chain will become separated entirely from the bicycle-system, littering the aisle between the tennis and cycling departments—here the crank-arm, no longer slowed by the system of which it was a part, will spin freely but without consequence to the velocity of the bicycle.

Here one finds that objects interact with other objects in definite ways even when all of the humans have gone home for the night. Furthermore, their interactions can be considered without being anthropomorphized. Harman explains how it "will be generally admitted that there is a sense in which even rocks confront other entities, whether by smashing or discoloring them" (p. 71). So now we turn to the analysis of objects insofar as they interact with other objects and subjects—that is, objects in their tool-being. Whitehead (1933/1967) provides a refreshing definition of how objects might be considered:

> Objects for an occasion can also be termed the 'data' for that occasion. The choice of terms entirely depends on the metaphor which you prefer. One word

carries the literal meaning 'lying in the way of', and the other word carries the literal meaning of 'being given to'. But both words suffer from the defect of suggesting that an occasion of experiencing arises out of a passive situation which is a mere welter of many data. (pp. 178-179)

Consistent with Heidegger's analysis of equipmentality, objects may be understood as occupying two modes of being. Objects could impede the becoming of various other subject-object events—that is, they could be understood as "lying in the way of" events; the broken chain seizing the drive-train-event. The very same object could also be absorbed into an event—that is, they could be understood as "being given to" an event as it unfolds; here the chain is completely enveloped, disappearing into the drive-train-event. While each of these modes of tool-being demands particular dimensions of a tool-being, neither exhausts the tool-being of its "real potentiality" to quote Whitehead from above. These instances of bicycle-chain tool-being suggest that it contributes only to the bicycle drive-train-event, and at all other times the bicycle chain withdraws from reality. This conception fails to recognize the reversibility characteristic of all modes of tool-being. Even when absorbed into the bicycle drivetrain, the bicycle chain's usefulness as a weapon, fashion accessory, or drivetrain-lubricant-distributor are not ready-to-hand but instantaneously lie dormant, present-at-hand. In order to rend the bicycle-chain tool-being's "real potentiality" from its absorption as ready-to-hand equipment to the drivetrain, a breakdown has to occur. Only then might its variety of potentialities be unleashed on the universe. These potentialities are always there, even when absorbed into the work of a subject. Thus the bicycle chain is both ready-to-hand as drivetrain-equipment and present-at-hand as a fashion accessory. This two-part structure of object-being is typical of all things. "Put as sharply as possible, there are only two principles at work in the cosmos: *Zu-* and *Vorhandenheit,* tool and broken tool. These never exist in isolation, but compose two dimensions of every object" (Harman, 2002/2006, p. 46). This means that behind even the most mundane present-at-hand characteristics of a given object lays unnavigable ontological depths. This is what Heidegger's analysis of the being that is characteristic of Dasein has yielded. We find here that this extends to objects as well. Rather than placing Dasein outside of Nature as the only being with ontological richness and depth, Harman observes that Dasein exemplifies tool-being in all objective forms. He writes,

Instead of human awareness on one side of the fence and colliding billiard balls on the other, we find that both of these realities belong on the same side of the fence. Even the mindless interaction of the eight ball and the nine ball will have to count as an instance of the *broken* tool. (p. 221)

Like the dual-subject in chapter six—liable to be swept up into either side of the prehending-prehended reversibility relationship—so too does one find a duality in objective tool-being. The ontological richness and depth that had originally been reserved for the being of humans, courtesy of Heidegger, has now been extended to all objects. There is no fissure that separates subjects from the objects they entertain; indeed, these both belong to the *flesh* of Nature.

This radical edge has extended the ontological and psychological depth traditionally reserved for humans and has applied it to bicycle crank-arms, baseball infields, and living-room lamps. The attempt stands as the first of its kind. As such, its effectiveness should be measured less in the immediate insights it supplies and more in the degree to which it extends the boundaries—albeit slightly—to that which seems acceptable as a psychological investigation. It may take a generation or two before an insightful OOP materializes.

# Future Directions

This project has re-examined the founding principles of humanistic psychology by reviewing the historical and scientific contexts out of which it grew. In its modern format, psychology is a logical empirical discipline that seeks to identity the physical and psychical bits that make up human behavior and experience. In this sense, it is reductive because it reduces human experience to the simplest bits and parts. This position has been criticized by a century of psychologists because it seems to miss out on something integral to psychology. In its humanistic format, psychology is a social, existential, or phenomenological discipline that seeks to identify the structures of human behavior and experience as they are lived. In this sense, it is holistic because the subject matter is always found within a greater context in which meaning is made. This position has only recently come under scrutiny due to its anthropocentric emphasis on the human. With a few exceptional areas of overlap, these two perspectives of the discipline of psychology remain divided.

Examples of nohumanist studies and posthumanist studies within the subdiscipline of humanistic psychology have been suggested. These reflect important areas of research that are currently ongoing in other fields. They are fields from which humanistic psychology would stand much to gain. Furthermore, their inclusion would be consistent with humanistic psychology's foundational axioms of openness of inquiry, and as proposed by Abraham Maslow, broadening the jurisdiction of psychology.

The radical edge of this line of inquiry, presented in the eighth and final chapter, suggests an ill-defined frontier. The conclusion here is *not* that an object-oriented psychology is necessarily impossible. Judgment is optimistically suspended on the possibility for such research programs. Indeed, the discipline of psychology would need to continue to undergo a transformation in order for such programs to develop. This transformation would begin with the increasing comfort regarding the recognition of nonhuman subjectivities and objectivities. With this shift in consciousness, methods like object-oriented psychology will continue to be applied in courageous and compelling ways that will lead to new insights. John Watson was earlier cited as an exemplar of Alfred North Whitehead's boldness in the generalization of metaphysical principles. Watson applied the rules of mechanism to humans and animals. By manipulating what occurs before behavior, Watson hypothesized that he could control behavior. This follows the mechanical law of cause and effect—namely, *if* cause, *then* effect. While his classical conditioning failed to yield the breakthroughs he had hoped, it opened up the door for the boldness of another behaviorist—B.F. Skinner. In a move that had to have been unthinkable at the time of Watson's *Behaviorism*, Skinner reversed the order of cause and effect. By following a target behavior with reinforcement, Skinner was able to increase the target behavior. As it stands with the present proposal for object-oriented psychology and alien phenomenology, the exciting work has yet to be done.

In summary, I have re-examined the founding principles of humanistic psychology by reviewing its original goals. The historical context out of which it emerged required that humanistic psychology reject certain areas of inquiry in order to advance a more meaningful program of research and practice. At the time, it was understood that such rejects were in service to a psychology that was more *humane*—or humanistic.

I have argued that humanistic psychology would benefit from an interdisciplinary dialogue with nonhumanism and posthumanism. Doing so would solve problems that have become increasingly apparent in the continued practice of humanistic psychology. Nonhuman studies demonstrate that human beings belong to a large category of complex, sophisticated life-forms that take part in constituting one-another through reciprocal interaction. These interactions may be understood through the principles of holism, intersubjectivity, and meaning. Posthuman studies demonstrate that the category of "human" has changed considerably. Rather than reject these changes as necessarily harmful ones, researchers may instead turn to the subject to understand just how these changes have occurred, and the consequences that have followed them.

## NONHUMAN DIRECTIONS FOR FUTURE RESEARCH

Up to this point the goal has been in describing how humanistic psychology would benefit by expanding the conception of its subject matter—namely, human being. Now it is time to suggest how humanistic psychology, once it has successfully expanded its definition of human being, can be insightful in interdisciplinary collaboration. Humanistic psychology does not need to be relegated to the margins of clinical and counseling psychologies, and the psychologies of motivation and personality as a blip on the map of psychology's historical development. I have found it useful today in a variety of settings outside the traditional hallways of humanistic psychology.

Minor traumatic brain injury rehabilitation. One approach to looking forward for directions of research is to start with some of humanistic psychologies governing principles and their creators. As described at length in Chapter 4, Kurt Goldstein was very keen on the natural processes of living organisms—a category to which humans belong. One such process—self-actualization—was of particular interest to humanistic psychologists such as Abraham Maslow and Fritz Perls. For Goldstein, self-actualization is a biological imperative that structure's an organism's world of meaning (defined as an *Umwelt* in the same chapter).

Goldstein believed that any symptom of pathology can be understood as a global organismic solution to a problem. Symptoms are not problems, but meaningful solutions to problems. As such, a symptom cannot be understood by itself, but must instead be viewed within the context of the organism within her environment. This approach worked particularly well with brain-injuries because it is always clear what the source of the problem is with such trauma, and subsequently how treatment might proceed.

The field of sport and exercise psychology is currently perplexed regarding the diagnosis and treatment of minor traumatic brain injuries such as concussions. That symptoms continue after all evidence of continued damage has dissipated is the puzzle known as Post-Concussion Syndrome (PCS). The classification itself indicates that the damage itself was temporary, taking only a few weeks to resolve (Coppel, 2014). Speculation has been made about the role of cerebral blood flow as well as autoregulation in the brain (Tan, Meehan, Iverson, and Taylor, 2014; Sviri and Newell, 2010). PCS athletes experience a number of symptoms when returning to exercise such as dizziness, nausea, and cognitive haze (Coppel, 2014). Another particularly biopsychosocial symptom is anxiety (Wood, McCane, Dawkins, 2011). The relationship between anxiety and these symptoms should be expected to students of Goldstein (1963) and Rollo May (2015). When viewing anxiety as the threat to one's existence, these symptoms may be understood as an unconscious way of avoiding a potentially catastrophic situation. The catastrophe may well be the lack of typical autoregulation in the nervous system. Tegeler, Tegeler, Cook, Lee, Gerdes, Shaltout, Miles, and Simpson (2016) explain how athletes who experience PCS symptoms also suffer from a lower heart-rate variability (HRV). HRV refers to the inconsistent beat of a heart. A heart that beats sixty times a minute does not beat once a second; there is variability in-between heart beats. This regular variance allows the cardiovascular system to respond to sudden changes in workload. PCS patients differ in that they miss out on this type of feedback. Tegeler et al. introduced an external source of biofeedback to these athletes so that they could actually hear the changes in their own brain activity by translating electrical frequencies into sonic frequencies through headphones. This procedure allows a person to regain their natural, biosemiotic capacity for dynamic adaptation. "Health," Tegeler et al. explain, "is a capacity for successful engagement with conditions of the natural environment, and the brain is the seat for orchestration of various system functions in concert" (p. 2).

Biofeedback is an area of mind-body research that has a long history in applied humanistic psychology research (Moss and Shaffer, 2016). It is just one of many insights that humanistic psychology could bring to the enigma that is PCS.

Humanistic psychologies of sport-performance. The 1970s saw a growth in the popularity of running. In addition to the gobs of people that began littering the roads, trails, and tracks, the popularity was also marked by an increase in the development of training principles. Over the decades that followed, the training of elite athletes became a matter of science. "Running" gets replaced by VO-2-Max training, lactate-threshold training, aerobic development, anaerobic development, fat-metabolizing runs, lactate-metabolizing runs, glycogen-metabolizing runs, etc.

After forty years of increasingly sophisticated scientific approaches to running, elite coach and former US marathoner John Kellogg (Kellogg, 2012) asks about what has really been gained. Instead of hooking his athletes up to heart-rate monitors and oxygen masks, Kellogg advocates a simplistic approach: running by feel. The notion is as old as is running, and the method couldn't be easier to employ. Kellogg explains that running should be like surfing—some days you spend all of your swimming out to sea, looking for the right wave; other days you find it easily and go for a ride. Running by feel allows the body to dictate intensity levels, duration, effort, rest, nutrition, etc., instead of relying on a chart of levels, times, and calories. When viewed from a nonhuman perspective such as a biosemiotic event, running by feel makes sense. This is to say that molecular processes within and around an individual are taking place in instantaneous, reciprocal, and meaningful ways. Consider a very basic intensity gauge: blood-lactate levels. When put to work, muscles produce lactate that can be converted to energy or cleared away as waste. Indeed, the very contraction of a muscle produces lactate. Thus, while walking or running, your leg-muscles produce lactate. If the intensity of a workout is high enough, muscles will produce more lactate than can be cleared away. This is experienced as burning sensation in your muscles. When the lactate build-up gets to a certain point, the workout ends or the intensity is adjusted in order for lactate clearance to catch back up. As one can imagine, there is a point between jogging and sprinting where the lactate production level begins to exceed the lactate-clearance rate. This is popularly called the lactate-threshold. The lactate threshold is of little consequence to sprinters because these races are typically done before lactate levels become unmanageable. The lactate threshold is of great consequence to long-distance runners. By spending time at the lactate threshold while in training, athletes can improve the efficiency with which lactate is removed from the muscles as well as increase their stamina for running through the discomfort.

As a staple in long-distance training regimens, lactate threshold workouts can be easy to overdo. By running these workouts too fast, overtraining can occur. By spending too much time beyond the lactate-threshold, allowing lactate to build up in the muscles, recovery can take considerably longer without any added fitness benefits. This makes the lactate threshold an incredibly important measurement.

Blood-lactate levels can be measured by taking a sample from a finger-prick test. When running close-to but below the lactate threshold, blood-lactate levels are low at about 2.0 mmols per liter of blood. Once the lactate threshold is exceeded, this level can jump to 4.0 mmols/liter. This jump occurs in a very small window when measured by a stopwatch, but a very large window when measured through perceived effort. For example, I can comfortably run at a pace of 5:50 minutes per mile, which is just below my lactate threshold. At this pace, my breathing is relaxed but steady, my form is comfortable, and my heart rate is about 85 percent HR-max. With sufficient nutrition, I could run at this pace for two or three hours. At a pace of 5:40 min/M, lactate begins to accumulate at a rate such that in an hour I will be forced to stop. At this pace, my breathing rate increases by 50 percent, extra effort is required to keep my form, and my heart rate is about 90 percent HR-max. And finally, at a pace of 5:30 min/M, lactate begins to accumulate rapidly. At this pace my breathing is stressed, my form is stressed, and my heart rate is about 92 percent HR-max.

Notice how in the above description, which is standard training protocol, all of the quantitative measures are close to one another. If measuring a workout by a heart rate monitor, 7 percent of HR-max (or about thirteen beats) is all that separates a workout that is too easy from one that is too hard. If measured by a stopwatch, then this difference is only twenties. Now consider the differences when measured by feel. Though only a few heartbeats per minute and a few seconds per mile separates lactate-clearance from lactate-accumulation, the difference in perceived effort is considerable.

This would be the place to start a *non*humanistic study of running by feel. It could have many different areas of investigation. For example, how easily can well-trained athletes approximate their own levels of effort that correspond to physiological adaptation principles? This would have the two-fold benefit of replacing stopwatch-based workouts, but also possibly drawing into question the direction of the relationship between perceived effort and blood-lactate levels. This might be followed by a phenomenological investigation of running at, below, or above the lactate threshold in a variety of contexts (e.g., it is famously easy to run at the lactate threshold for six miles in a race, but infamously difficult to run these six miles alone while during a workout).

These would provide the beginning of a research program that emphasizes running by feel. Training by heart-rate monitor and stopwatch might be replaced by running by feel. The science of running would slowly incorporate the phenomenology of running, and runners would not have to seek micromanagement for running mechanics, nutrition, pace, gait, rest, etc., because these are less standardized than they are personal.

All of this says nothing about the role played by proprioceptive processes—or the awareness of bodies in space, which seems to occur more on the level of molecular feedback loops than conscious awareness. As Hoffmeyer explains, "proprioceptive information is more important than vision when the task is to direct a correct movement such as reaching out for something" (p. 232).

## POSTHUMAN DIRECTIONS FOR FUTURE RESEARCH

Chapters 6 and 7 have demonstrated how influential technology has been in shaping human beings, perception, history, and social relations. Rather than view these with a critical or pessimistic eye, humanistic psychology could continue its program of fidelity to the subject. The best way to understand *how* technology has shaped our relationships is to ask people about it.

Humanistic cyberpsychology. As it stands, postphenomenology remains an analytic project. Their goal is to explain how the structure of tools and programs opens certain possibilities while foreclosing others. Humanistic psychology could make this an empirical one. When Sherry Turkle (2012) describes how her daughter found the animatronic robots more *real* than the dolphins and whales at Sea World, she lets out a disheartened sigh. But this provides an excellent opportunity to learn more about how "real" has changed. There could very well be an existential ethic in there that has been smuggled in through entertainment and technology that is influencing how Turkle's daughter judges her own behavior.

Social media is changing the fabric of human interaction and communication, not to mention the humans themselves. With a lack of devoted study, these important factors in the human lifeworld are at risk of being subsumed by pseudo-study and fake news. *Has Instagram usage contributed to deficits in self-esteem?* Humanistic psychologists can examine how this media platform is used, and, if applicable, how the consequences of its abuse can be avoided. With the rapid proliferation of media platforms, there will always be something new to examine.

How might students feel more engaged in an online classroom? What contributes to a personal atmosphere in an online class? Is it possible to great a learner-centered space online? Rather than reject the possibility of a meaningful classroom experience in online education, humanistic psychologists can begin exploring these as new possibilities. Moreover, this can be an opportunity to great instructional content where there is precious little. The growth of online course-availability has not been matched by the availability of online course materials by experts in the field. Unless something changes, there will be an entire generation of undergraduate students who learn their psychology from freely available videos produced by website owners that lack discipline-specific credentials. Humanistically inclined psychology instructors could take advantage of this gap in availability and produce content to be used in classrooms around the world, as well as introduce new learner-centered teaching styles in the online classroom where no real consensus has yet been found.

As a corollary to online instruction, there is also the potential topic of online therapy. To be sure, such platforms of therapy will no doubt be different from the traditional face-to-face platforms, but need these differences only be negative? In addition to accessibility, what are some of the advantages of nonlocal therapy? How might these advantages be used to improve face-to-face therapies? Instead of seeing growth in the area of cyberpsychology as a loss of something important, humanistic psychologists can take advantage of the opportunity to explore how this growth is accompanied by a gain in something important—and they can be the ones to find it because they are not afraid to investigate these from the subject's perspective.

My hope is that this re-examination of the founding principles of humanistic psychology and subsequent foray into its future possibilities will strengthen the subdiscipline as a whole. There is little doubt in my mind that there is still a great deal of work to be done in shaping the future of nonhumanism and posthumanism in humanistic psychology. For these related disciplines to be truly and earnestly integrated together, it is going to take a scholar who has been educated and trained within a discipline where such a possibility has never been rejected. Her curiosity will not have been directed away from certain scientific assumptions, or steered afield of biology, zoology, and medicine. She will be able to ask questions that might even make us, as a humanistic psychological collective, a bit uncomfortable. In short, it will take someone as insightful, as courageous, and as inspired as Abraham Maslow, who helped change the way psychologists understand what it means to be human.

# References

Abram, D. (1996). *Spell of the senuous: Perception and language in a more-than-human world.* New York: Vintage.

Adams, W. W. (2006). "The ivory-billed woodpecker, ecopsychology, and the crisis of extinction: On annihilating and nurturing other beings, relationships, and ourselves." *The Humanistic Psychologist, 34(2),* 111-133.

Adams, W. W. (2015). "Healing our dissociation from body and nature: Gestalt, Levinas, and earth's ethical call." *British Gestalt Journal, 24(1),* 32-38.

Anthony, C. (1995). "Ecopsychology and the deconstruction of whiteness." In T. Rozsak, M.E. Gomes, and A.D. Kanner (Eds.)., *Ecopsychology: Restoring the earth: Healing the mind,* 263-278. San Francisco: Sierra Club Books.

Applebaum, D. (1993). *Everyday spirits.* Albany, NY: SUNY Press.

Baars, B. (1986). *The cognitive revolution in psychology.*

Bains, P. (2005). "Subjectless subjectivities." In B. Massumi (Ed.), *Shock to thought: Expression after Deleuze and Guattari,* 101-116. New York: Routledge. (Original work published in 2002)

Baker (2013) transpersonal methods).

Barbaras, R. (2004). *The being of the phenomenon: Merleau-Ponty's ontology.* T. Toadvine and L. Lawlor (Trans.). Bloomington, IN: Indiana University Press. (Original text published in 1991).

Bogost, I. (2012). *Alien phenomenology, or what it's like to be a thing.* Minneapolis, MN: Minnesota University Press.

Boring, E. (1953). "A history of introspection." *Psychological Bulletin, 50(3),* 169-189.

Braidotti, Rosi. 2013. *The Posthuman.* Malden, MA: Polity Press.

Braud, W., and Anderson, R. (1998). *Transpersonal research methods for the social sciences: Honoring human experience.* Thousand Oaks, CA: SAGE.

Bryant, L., Srnicek, N., Harman, G. (2011). *The speculative turn: Continental materialism and realism.* Melbourne, AUS: re.press.

Caplan (2013). 400 amazing Facebook statistics and facts. http://expandedramblings.com/index.php/by-the-numbers-17-amazing-facebook-stats/#.VEapzvnF-So. Accessed October 21, 2014.

Cobb, J. B. (2001). "Deep ecology and process thought." *Process Studies, 30(1),* 112-131.

Cobb, J. B., and Griffin, D. R. (1977). *Mind in nature: Essays on the interface of science and philosophy.* Washington, DC: University Press of America.

Cohen, R.S., and Wartofsky, M.W. (1980). Editorial Preface, in H. Maturana and F. Varela, *Autopoiesis and cognition: Realization of the living,* R.S. Cohen and M.W. Wartofsky (Eds.), v-vi. Dortrecht: D. Reidel Publishing.

Coppel, D. (2014). Post-concussion syndrome. In G.T. Brown (Ed.), *Mind, body, and sport: Understanding and supporting student-athlete mental wellness*, 65-68. Indianapolis, IN: NCAA Publications.

Crick, F. (1995). *Astonishing hypothesis: The scientific search for the soul.* New York: Scribner. (Original work published in 1994).

Deleuze, G. (1988). *Spinoza: Practical Philosophy.* San Francisco, CA: City Lights Books. (Original work published in 1970).

Diamond, J. (1992). *The third chimpanzee: The evolution and future of the human animal.* New York: HarperCollins Publishers, Inc.

Dillon, M.C. (1998). *Merleau-Ponty's ontology.* Evanston, IL: Northwestern University Press. (Original work published in 1988).

Emmeche, C., and Kull, K. (2011). *Towards a semiotic biology: Life is the action of signs.* London: Imperial College Press.

Fisher, A. (2013). *Radical ecopsychology: Psychology in the service of life.* Albany, NY: SUNY Press.

Fromm, E., Suzuki, D. T., and deMartino, R., (1960). *Zen Buddhism and psychoanalysis.* New York: Harper & Brothers.

Goldberg, E. (2009). *The new executive brain: Frontal lobes in a complex world.* New York: Oxford University Press.

Goldstein, K. (1995). *The organism: A holistic approach to biology derived from pathological data in man.* Boston, MA: Zone Books. (Original text published in 1934)

Griffin, D.R. (1977). Whitehead's philosophy and some general notions of physics and biology. In Cobb and Griffin (Eds.), *Mind in nature: The interface of science and philosophy.* Lanham, MD: University Press of America.

Grusin, R. (2015). *The nonhuman turn.* Minneapolis, MN: Minnesota University Press.

Hameroff, Kazniak, and Scott. (1997). Conference proceedings.

Hamrick, W.S. (1999). "A process view of the flesh: Whitehead and Merleau-Ponty." *Process Studies, 28(1-2),* 117-129.

Hamrick, W.S. (2012). *Nature and logos: A Whiteheadian key to Merleau-Ponty's fundamental thought.* Albany, NY: SUNY Press.

Harman, G. (2005). *Guerilla metaphysics: Phenomenology and the carpentry of things.* Chicago, IL: Open Court.

Harman, G. (2006) *Tool-being: Heidegger and the metaphysics of objects.* Chicago, IL: Open Court. (Original work published in 2002).

Harman, G. (2010). "A theory of objects in Whitehead and Heidegger." In G. Harman (Ed.). *Towards speculative realism: Essays and lectures.* Washington, DC: zero books. 2010.

Harman, G. (2011). *Quentin Meillassoux: Philosophy in the making.* Edinburgh, UK: Edinburgh University Press.

Harper, S. (1995). "The way of the wilderness." In T. Rozsak, M. E. Gomes, and A. D. Kanner (Eds.)., *Ecopsychology: Restoring the earth: Healing the mind,* 183-200. San Francisco: Sierra Club Books.

Hartshorne, C. (1977). "Physics and psychics: The place of mind in nature." In J. B. Cobb and D. R. Griffin, (Eds.). *Mind in nature: The interface of science and philosophy.* 89-96. Lanham, MD: University Press of America.

Heidegger, M. (1962). *Being and time.* J. Macquarrie and E. Robinson (Eds.) New York: Harper Perennial. (Original work published in 1927).

Heidegger, M. (1966). *Discourse on thinking.* J. M. Anderson and E. H. Freud, (Trans.). New York: Harper Perennial.

Heidegger, M. (1977). "Modern science, mathematics, and metaphysics." In *Basic Writings,* DF Krell (Ed.). New York: Harper & Row. (Original work published in 1967).

Hillman, J. (1995). "A psyche the size of the earth: A psychological foreward." In T. Rozsak, M. E. Gomes, and A. D. Kanner (Eds.)., *Ecopsychology: Restoring the earth: Healing the mind,* xvii-xxiii. San Francisco: Sierra Club Books.

Hoffmeyer, J. (2015). "Semiotic individuation and Ernst Cassirer's challenge." *Progress in biophysics and molecular biology, 119,* 607-615.

Hoffmeyer, J. (2014). "Semiotic scaffolding: A biosemiotic link between sema and soma." In K. R. Cabell and J. Valsiner (Eds.), *The catalyzing mind: Beyond models of causality*, 95-110. New York: Springer.

Hoffmeyer, J. (2008). *Biosemiotics: An examination into the signs of life and the life of signs.* Scranton, PA: University of Scranton Press. (Original work published in Danish, 2003).

Husserl, E. (2002). *Ideas: General introduction to pure phenomenology.* W.R. Boyce Gibson (Trans.) New York: Routledge.

Husserl, E. (1970). *The crisis in European sciences and transcendental phenomenology.* D. Carr (Trans.) Evanston, IL: Northwestern University Press.

Ihde, Don (1990). *Technology and the lifeworld: From garden to earth.* Bloomington, IN: University of Indiana Press.

James, W. (2007). *Principles of psychology. Vol. I,II.* New York: Cosimo Classics. (Original work published in 1890).

James, W. (1962). *Talks to teachers on psychology and to students on some of life's ideals.* Mineola, NY: Dover Publications, Inc. (Original work published in 1899).

Kellogg, J. (2012). The updated training wisdom of John Kellogg J. Davis (Ed.) Unpublished manuscript. http://www.runningwritings.com/2012/04/updated-training-wisdom-of-john-kellogg.html. Accessed June 12, 2015.

Koch, C. (2012). *Consciousness.* Boston, MA: The MIT Press.

Köhler, W. (1957). *Gestalt psychology.* New York: Liveright Publishing Company. (Original work published in 1947).

Koffka, K. (1922). Perception: An introduction to the *Gestalt-theorie. Psychological Bulletin* 19, 531-585.

Kohn, Alfie (1993). *Punished by Rewards.* Boston, MA: Houghton Mifflin.

Krippner, S. (1991). Foreword. In C. M. Aanstoos (Ed.), *Studies in Humanistic Psychology*, vi-viii. Carrolton, GA: West Georgia College.

Kuhn, T.S. (2012). *Structure of scientific revolutions* (4th ed.). Chicago, IL: University of Chicago Press. (Original work published in 1962).

Lanier, J. (2009). *You are not a gadget: A manifesto.* New York: Random House.

Lashley, K. S. (1930). "Basic neural mechanisms in behavior." *Psychological Review, 37,* 1-24.

Leclerc, I. (1977). "Some main philosophical issues involved in contemporary scientific thought." In J. B. Cobb and D. R. Griffin, (Eds.). *Mind in nature: The interface of science and philosophy.* 101-108. Lanham, MD: University Press of America.

Libet, B. (1985). Unconscious cerebral initiative and the role of conscious will in voluntary action. *The Behavioral and Brain Sciences. 8, 529-566.*

Lloyd, G. (1996). *Routledge philosophy guide to Spinoza and the ethics.* New York: Routledge.

Maslow, A. (1966). *The psychology of science: A reconnaissance.* Chicago, IL: Henry Regnery Company.

Maslow, A. (1968). *Toward a psychology of being.* New York: D. Van Nostrand Company. (Original work published in 1962).

Maslow, A. (1976). *The farther reaches of human nature.* New York: Penguin. (Original work published in 1972).

Massumi, B. (1995). "Autonomy and affect." *Cultural Critique, 31,* 83-109.

Maturana, H., and Varela, F. (1972). *Autopoiesis and cognition: The realization of the living.* Boston, MA: D. Reidel Publishing Company.

May, R. (2015). *The meaning of anxiety.* New York: W.W. Norton & Co.

Mazis, G.A. (2008). *Humans, animals, and robots: Blurring boundaries.* Albany, NY: SUNY Press.

Meillassoux, Q. (2012). *After finitude: An essay on the necessity of contingency.* R. Brassier (Trans.). London: Bloomsburg. (Original work published in 2006).

Merleau-Ponty, M. (1962). *Phenomenology of perception.* (C. Smith, Trans.), New York: The Humanities Press. (Original work published in 1945).

Merleau-Ponty, M. (1963). *Structure of Behavior.* A.L. Fisher (Trans.). Pittsburgh, PA: Duquesne University Press. (Original text published in 1942).

Merleau-Ponty, M. (1968). *The visible and the invisible.* In C. Lefort (Ed.), A. Lingis (Trans.). Evanston, IL: Northwestern University Press. (Original work published in 1964).

Merleau-Ponty, M. (2003). *Nature: Course notes from the Collège de France*. R. Vallier, (Trans.). Evanston, IL: Northwestern University Press. (Original work prepared in 1956-60).

Morton, T. (2013). *Hyperobjects: Philosophy and ecology after the end of the world*. Minneapolis, MN: University of Minnesota Press.

Moss, D., and Shaffer, F. (2016). *Foundations of heart-rate variability biofeedback: A book of readings*. Wheat Ridge, CO: Association for Applied Psychophysiology and Biofeedback.

Noë, A. (2009). *Out of our heads: Why you are not your brain and other stories from the biology of consciousness*. New York: Hill & Wang.

Ortega y Gasset, J. (1961). *History as a system: And other essays toward a philosophy of history*. New York: WW Norton & Company.

Pantin, C.F.A. (1968). *The relations between the sciences*. London: Cambridge University Press.

Parkinson, G.H.R. (2000). Editor's Introduction. In Spinoza, *Ethics*. G.H.R. Parkinson (Ed., Trans.), 5-50. Oxford: Oxford University Press.

Perls, F. (1972). *In and out the garbage pail*. New York: Bantam.

Polanyi, M. (1958). *Personal knowledge*. Chicago, IL: The University of Chicago Press.

Polanyi, M. (1964). *Science, faith, and society*. Chicago, IL: The University of Chicago Press.

Polkinghorne, D. (1982). *Methodology for the human sciences: Systems of inquiry*. Albany, NY: State University of New York Press.

Ramachandran (2011). *The tell-tale brain*. New York: Norton.

Ravven, H. M. (2003). "Spinozistic approaches to evolutionary naturalism: Spinoza's anticipation of contemporary affective neuroscience." *Politics and the Life Sciences, 22(1)*. 70-74.

Rogers, Carl (1961). *On becoming a person: A therapist's view of psychotherapy*. New York: Houghton Mifflin.

Romanyshyn, R. (1982). *Psychological life: From science to metaphor*. Austin, TX: University of Texas Press.

Rosen, S. (2008). *Self-evolving universe: A phenomenological approach to nature's unity in diversity*. Hackensack, NJ: World Scientific Publishing Co.

Rosen, S. (2015). "Why natural science needs phenomenological philosophy." *Progress in Biophysics and Molecular Biology, 119*, 257-269.

Rosenberger, R., and Verbeek, P. (2015). *Phenomenological investigations: Essays on human-technology relations*. Lanham, MD: Lexington Books.

Ruyer, R. (1966). *Paradoxes de la conscience et limites de l'automatisme*. Paris: Albin Michel.

Satel, S., and Lilienfeld, S. (2013). *Brainwashed: The seductive appeal of mindless neuroscience*. New York: Basic Books.

Schrödinger, E. (1967). *What is life? The physical aspect of the living cell*. Cambridge, UK: Cambridge University Press. (Original work published in 1944).

Seung, S. (2012). *Connectome: How the brain's wiring makes who we are*. Boston, MA: Houghton Mifflin Harcourt.

Shaviro, S. (2012). *Without criteria: Kant, Whitehead, Deleuze, and aesthetics*. Cambridge, MA: The MIT Press.

Simeonov, P., Rosen, S. A., and Gare, A. (2015). "Special theme issue on integral biomathics: Life sciences, mathematics, and phenomenological philosophy. *Progress in Biophysics and Molecular Biology, 119*.

Skinner, B.F. (1971). *Beyond freedom and dignity*. New York: Bantam.

Sparrow, T. (2014). *The end of phenomenology: Metaphysics and the new realism*. Edinburgh: Edinburgh University Press.

Sparrow, T. (2015). *Plastic bodies: Rebuilding sensation after phenomenology*. London: Open Humanities Press.

Spinoza, B. (1995). *The chief works of Benedict de Spinoza*. R.H.M. Elwes (Trans.). New York: Dover. (Original text published in 1883).

Spinoza, B. (2000). *Ethics*. GHR Parkinson (Ed., Trans.). Oxford, UK: Oxford University Press.

Stanovich, Keith. 2012. *How to think straight about psychology*. 10th Ed. Edinburgh: Pearson.

Stapp, H. P. (2011). *Mindful universe: Quantum mechanics and the participating observer*. New York: Springer.

Stengers, I. (2012). *Thinking with Whitehead*. Cambridge, MA: Harvard University Press.

Stenner, Paul (2011). James and Whitehead: Assemblage and Systemization of a Deeply Empiricist Mosaic Philosophy. *European Journal of Pragmatism and American Philosophy* 3(1), 101-139.

Tan, C.O.; Meehan, W.P.; Iverson, G.L.; Taylor, J.A. (2014). Cerebrovascular regulation, exercise, and mild traumatic brain injury. *Neurology*, 83, 1665-1672.

Tegeler, C.H.; Tegeler, C.L.; Cook, J.F.; Lee, S.W.; Gerdes, L.; Shaltout, H.A.; Miles, C.M.; Simpson, S.L. (2016). A preliminary study of the effectiveness of an allostatic, closed-loop, acoustic stimulation neurotechnology in the treatment of athletes with persisting post-concussion symptoms. *Sports Medicine*, 2(39), 1-8.

Thorpe, W. H. (1977). "The frontiers of biology: Does process thought help?" In J. B. Cobb and D. R. G. Cobb, (Eds.), *Mind in nature: The interface of science and philosophy*, 1-11. Lanham, MD: University Press of America.

Titchener, E. B., (1912). "The schema of introspection." *American journal of psychology, 23,* 485-508.

Toulmin, S., and Leary, D. (1985). "The cult of empiricism in psychology." In S. Koch and D. Leary, (Eds.). *A century of psychology as a science,* 594-617. New York: McGraw-Hill.

Turkle, S. (2012). *Alone together: Why we expect more from technology and less from each other.* New York: Basic Books.

Varela, F. (1996). "Neurophenomenology: A methodological remedy for the hard problem." *Journal of Consciousness Studies, 3,* 330-349.

Watson, J. (1930). *Behaviorism.* New York: W. W. Norton & Co.

Wertheimer, M. (1938). "Laws of organization in perceptual forms." In W. Ellis, (Ed., Trans.). *A source book of gestalt psychology* (pp 71-88). London: Routledge and Kegan Paul. [psychclassics.yorku.ca].

Whitehead, A.N. (1953). *Science and the modern world.* New York: Free Press. (Original text published in 1925).

Whitehead, A.N. *Adventures of Ideas.* (1967). New York: Free Press. (Original text published in 1933).

Whitehead, A.N. (1978). *Process and reality, corrected ed.* New York: Free Press.

Whitehead, A.N. (2012). *The concept of nature.* Lexington, KY: Create Space Independent Publishing Platform. (Original work published in 1920).

Whitehead, P.M. (in press). "Goldstein's concept of self-actualization: A biosemiotic view." *The Humanistic Psychologist.*

Whitehead, P.M. (2015). "Overcoming parallelism: Naturalizing phenomenology with Goldstein and Merleau-Ponty." *Progress in Biophysics and Molecular Biology, 119,* 502-509.

Whitehead, P.M. (2014). "Contemporary neuroscience humanizes: A look at cortical bi-lateral asymmetry and how it got that way." *Humanistic Psychologist, 42(2).* 121-136.

Whitehead, P.M. (2013). "The effects of student-centered learning on problem solving abilities: A neurobiological consideration." Paper presented at the *South East Philosophy of Education Society Conference.* St. Petersburg, FL. February 1-2.

Wolfe, C. (2009). *What is posthumanism?* Minneapolis, MN: Minnesota University Press.

Wood, R.L.; McCabe, M.; and Dawkins, J. (2011). The role of anxiety sensitivity in symptom perception after minor head injury: An exploratory study. *Brain Injury,* 25(13-14), 1296-1299.

Wundt, W.M. (1897). *Outlines of psychology.* C. H. Judd (Trans.). Toronto, ON: York University Psychology Classics.

# Index

Maslow, Abraham, 5, 7, 13, 16, 19, 21–24, 26–31
Mazis, Glen. *See* Embodiment of technology
mechanics, mechanism, 1, 3, 15, 22, 31, 36, 40, 67
Merleau-Ponty, Maurice, 25, 35–37, 38, 39–40, 40–41, 44–48, 122, 125, 131, 143–146. *See also* embodiment, flesh
Morton, Tim, 119. *See also* hyperobjects

neurophenomenology, 84
neuroscience, 25; associationism. *See* Lashley, Karl; Spinoza's neuroscience; Spinoza, Baruch
Newtonian mechanics. *See* mechanics, mechanism
Noë, Alva, 24–25, 79–81
nonhuman, nonhumanism, 12–13, 70, 96; nonhuman subjectivity. *See* subjectivity

object, ix, 8, 25, 30, 42, 49, 51, 61–62, 65, 133–135, 141–142; Heidegger's objects, 142–143; Merleau-Ponty's objects, 143–146; tool-being. *See* Harman, Graham
object-oriented ontology, OOO, 11, 115, 128
objectivity, 22, 62

panpsychism, panpsychic, 50, 128, 132
Perls, Fritz, 16, 31

phenomenology. *See* Martin Heidegger, Maurice Merleau-Ponty, Edmund Husserl, postphenomenology
Polanyi, Michael, 22–24
post-concussion syndrome, 153
posthumanism, 9
posthumanities, 8–12, 30
postphenomenology, 111–115
prehension, 60, 61, 88, 125

Rosen, Steven, 14

self-actualization, 7, 17, 30–32
Skinner, B.F. *See* behaviorism
social media, 102–104
speculative realism, 116, 127
Spinoza, Baruch, 15, 71; bi-directional causality. *See* causality; immanence, 75; neuroscience, 81
Stapp, Henry, 127
subject, 23, 51, 53, 59, 79, 88, 123
subjectivity, 25, 60, 80, 87, 119; nonhuman, 93–99; posthuman, 37

technology, 31, 101, 111, 156. *See also* iPhone, AI
tool-being. *See* Harman, Graham
Turkle, Sherri, 31, 103, 104, 156

Watson, John. *See* behaviorism
Whitehead, Alfred North, 41, 67, 88, 125, 141. *See also* prehension
Wundt, Wilhelm, 2, 128

# About the Author

Patrick M. Whitehead is an assistant professor of psychology at Albany State University. He is the author of *Psychologizing: A Personal, Practice-Based Approach to Psychology* (Rowman & Littlefield, 2017), and *Education in a Post-Factual World: From Knowing to Understanding* (BrownWalker Press, forthcoming). Patrick's work has been published in *The Humanistic Psychologist*, the *Journal of Phenomenological Psychology*, and the *Indo-Pacific Journal of Phenomenology*.